NARRATIVE

OF

THE MUTINIES IN OUDE

(COMPILED FROM AUTHENTIC RECORDS)

NARRATIVE

OF

THE MUTINIES IN OUDE

(COMPILED FROM AUTHENTIC RECORDS)

BY

CAPTAIN G. HUTCHINSON

GYAN

Published by

Gyan Publishing House
5, Ansari Road
Daryaganj, New Delhi-110002
Phone: 011-47034999, 9811692060
E-mail: books@gyanbooks.com

Distribution Network
gyanbooks.com
India, USA, Canada, UK, Australia

ISBN: 978-93-6433-301-6 (HB
First Published, 1859

2nd Impression 2024

Printed at: Gyan Press, Delhi.

NARRATIVE OF THE MUTINIES IN OUDE
Author: CAPTAIN GHUTCHINSON

NARRATIVE

OF

THE MUTINIES IN OUDE.

COMPILED FROM AUTHENTIC RECORDS,

BY

CAPTAIN G. HUTCHINSON,

BENGAL ENGINEERS,

MILITARY SECRETARY TO THE CHIEF COMMISSIONER, OUDE.

PUBLISHED BY AUTHORITY.

LONDON:

SMITH, ELDER & CO., 65, CORNHILL.

M.DCCC.LIX.

PREFACE.

THIS Narrative has been compiled with the concurrence of the Government of India, and by the direction of R. Montgomery, Esq., C.S., Chief Commissioner of Oude, with the object of affording to all who may have lost friends or relations in Oude the most accurate and complete information that the Local Government has been able to collect.

The utmost care and research have been taken to draw from all sources any information tending to throw light on the deeds and sufferings of our countrymen and women during that eventful period.

Narrators have, as much as possible, been left to tell their own story in their own words, a few necessary links only being supplied here and there as they appeared necessary.

The following officers have supplied valuable information:—

C. Wingfield, Esq., C. S., late Commissioner, Baraitch Division, Oude.
Major Carnegie, late City Magistrate, Lucknow.
Captain Reid, late Deputy Commissioner, Fyzabad.
Major Barrow, late Deputy Commissioner, Selone.

S. Martin, Esq., C. S., late Deputy Commissioner, Lucknow.
Captain Alexander Orr, late Assist. Commissioner, Fyzabad.
Captain Adolphus Orr, late Oude Police.
Captain Bunbury, late Oude Police.
Captain John Hearsey, late Oude Police.
Lieut. Meecham, late 7th Oude Irregular Infantry.
Lieut. E. E. Clark, late Assistant Commissioner, Gonda.
Mr. E. Bickers, late Setapore Commissioner's Office.
Mr. E. Phillips, late Setapore Deputy Commissioner's Office.
Mr. E. Dudman, late Setapore Deputy Commissioner's Office.
Mr. Durand, late Mulaon Deputy Commissioner's Office.
Mr. D. Gruyther, late Derriabad Commissioner's Office.

G. Hutchinson, Captain,
Military Secretary to the Chief Commissioner, Oude.

Lucknow, 1*st May*, 1857.

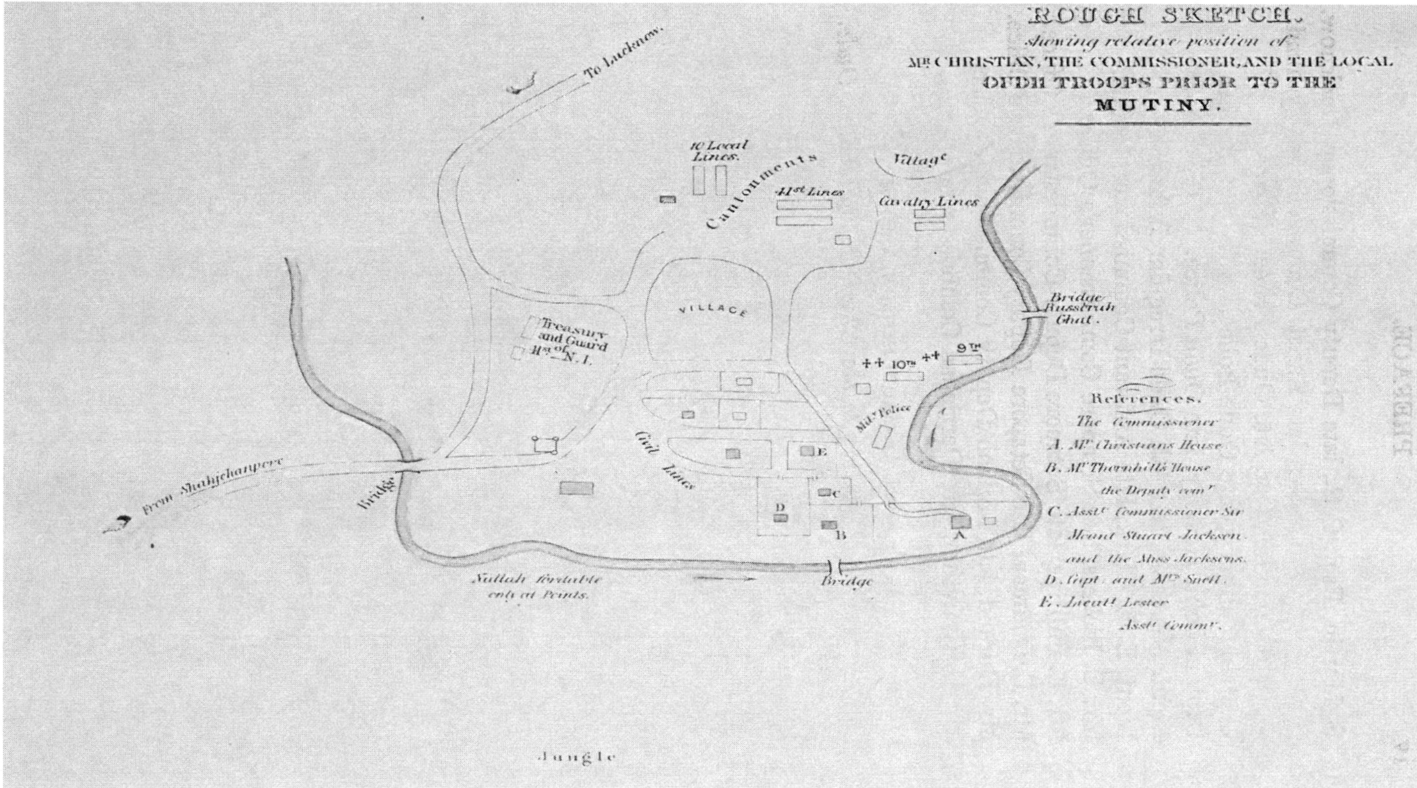
ROUGH SKETCH,
showing relative position of
Mr. CHRISTIAN, THE COMMISSIONER, AND THE LOCAL
OUDH TROOPS PRIOR TO THE
MUTINY.
To Lucknow.
10 Local Lines.
Cantonments
Village
41st Lines
Cavalry Lines
VILLAGE
Treasury and Guard 41st of N. I.
Bridge Russtrah Ghat.
++ 10th ++ 9th
Milty Police
Civil Lines
From Shahjehanpore
Bridge
Nullah fordable only at Points.
Bridge
Jungle
References.
The Commissioner
A. Mr. Christians House.
B. Mr. Thornhill's House the Deputy comr.
C. Asstt. Commissioner Sir Mount Stuart Jackson and the Miss Jacksons.
D. Capt. and Mrs. Snell.
E. Lieutt. Lester Asstt. Commr.

NARRATIVE

OF

EVENTS IN OUDE,

IN CONNECTION WITH

THE MUTINY OF 1857.

THAT a correct appreciation may be formed of the effect of the mutiny in Oude, it is necessary to consider its state before that infectious scourge swept over it.

The dynasty of Oude was founded in 1711, by Nawab Mahomed Ameen, better known as Saadut Khan Boorhân-ool Moolk.

Succeeding governors were styled nawabs from 1739 to 1819, and kings from 1819 to 6th February 1856.

Ghazeeooddeen Hyder, the ruler of Oude in 1819, received in that year, from the British Government, the title of king.

From the first establishment of a governor, the system of government has been nearly the same.

The governor, as supreme, had his court of justice apparently open to all appellants, rich or poor, whilst the vizeer, or prime minister, held a similar subordinate court.

The punishment of death could only be passed by the governor, and if the subject was a Mahomedan, the concurrence of the Mahomedan high priest was necessary.

The city governor or kotwal held a court for minor cases occurring in the capital (Lucknow), and the residents of each district received their meed of justice from the hands of that individual to whom the revenues of the district were farmed; these men were styled chuckladars, and their power of oppression was, in reality, unlimited.

From the above it will be seen that the only appeal against the oppression of a chuckladar, *alias* district governor, was to the vizeer or to the king, and the difficulties attendant on that appeal may be well conceived by any one who is at all acquainted with the Asiatic character, or who considers that these chuckladars took the contracts of their districts year by year, and necessarily, being the *bonâ fide* creatures of the minister, or of any individual who at that time swayed the king, always had a friend at court ready so to crush or stifle the voice of complaint, that but a suffocated whisper, if even that, could ever reach the king's presence.

Such were the principal apparent upholders of justice in Oude: the king, the vizeer, the city magistrate, and the chuckladars; and it will be necessary to narrate how they carried on their various duties, for the right conception of the state of Oude at the annexation.

The king, Wajid Ally Shah, occupant of the throne of Oude, ascended the throne on the death of his father, Umjud Ally Shah, and at first made some effort to transact business. Very soon he acquiesced in the joint suggestion of his minister and creatures, that such work, such inquiry, such laborious perusal of documents, was as unnecessary as it was unsuited to the light of the universe; but that cases might be heard within the presence, and his majesty could order the seal of State to be appended to the decisions of infinite wisdom.

Too soon this last act dropped into disuse, and the seal of State was made over to the minister together with the wisdom it would confirm, and thus the king virtually ceased either to administer justice himself to his people or even to witness its administration in his presence.

It must not be supposed that the influence of the king, for good or evil, ceased with his withdrawal from public administration; on the contrary, for the latter it increased tenfold.

Applicants who yet sought justice from their far too honoured king had to wade through a sea of bribery, thick with the filthy avariciousness of eunuchs, fiddlers, dancing girls, prostitutes, and other equally low characters, too numerous to detail. In addition to these creatures around him, the king had four wives by marriage according to Mahomedan law, and twenty-nine acknowledged wives by "Motah," and four hundred female attendants called "Motah" wives, but not permanently united as the others.

This "Motah" was a ceremony invented for convenience, and was as binding as a lawful marriage for the period it embraced; namely, three hours, or three days, or three months, or three years. At the expiration of the Motah agreement either party was free to marry whom they fancied.

The power of the king thus surrounded was exercised first by the favourite begum or wife, and secondly, by the favourite attendants from amongst the motley crowds. Before these the minister bowed in helpless resignation, and failed not to remember that a chuckladar's contract must include the favourite begum's proper *douceur*. So completely was this matter of fact that chuckladars often could not get their contracts until the begum's *douceur* was paid in full or part.

It will be seen from the above how completely the king sought only his own pleasure, to the utter neglect of his people, and that *that* good-nature, love of ease, and abandonment to pleasure,—which even in lesser individuals is but falsely styled harmless,—became in the king a crime which, rendering all things venal, drew alike from justice and prostitution the means of gratifying himself and those around him.

As we descend in the scale of government, we find a prime minister; a financial minister; a paymaster-general; an assistant to the prime minister; a meer moonshee, who carried on the correspondence between the king and the British government; a superintendent of the dewan of the king; a superintendent of the dewan of the vizeer; a treasurer in charge of the crown jewels and private moneys of the king; a treasurer in charge of government treasury; a superintendent of city police; a kotwal, or magistrate of the city; a superintendent of magazines and commissariat; three principal physicians; a poet and aide-de-camp; a superintendent of city news; and a superintendent of district news. Such were the principal individuals permanently attached to the court, with many others of minor importance.

At the period of annexation Allee Nuckee Khan was prime minister on a salary of ten thousand rupees a month; Maharajah Balkishen was financier on five thousand; all others had salaries, no doubt meant to be nominal, the perquisites providing the ways and means for those splendid displays of elephants, horses, &c., in which the court attendants loved to indulge. The average salary of all, from the paymaster-general to the poet, did not actually exceed three hundred rupees a month, their expenses being more like three thousand.

The minister was not a man whose character was esteemed, and in his light the financial minister, Maharajah Balkishen, showed to advantage, particularly in his later years.

The wife of the prime minister entirely ruled him, and as the king had deputed all business to him, so he deputed all he possibly could, nominally, to his darogah, but virtually to Moonshee Mahomed Hoossain, who naturally, in concert with the prime minister's wife, held very great power. He entirely superseded the court of Dewan Aum, or the court to which cases of appeal to, and orders from, the king were nominally sent.

Maharajah Balkishen was of the kaeth, or writer caste. He was probably the least corrupt of all the durbar officials. He was a good man of business, labouring incessantly. His memory was remarkable. The regular salary of the maharajah was five thousand rupees per mensem, but his perquisites (allowed and fixed by the late king, Umjud Ally Shah) were very large. His nuzzeranah, or presents, from all districts amounted to six lacs of rupees per annum; on this enormous sum the king levied ten annas per rupee, leaving the maharajah a net sum of rupees two lacs and twenty-five thousand. It may be interesting to note here that the maharajah died shortly before the final capture of Lucknow; he had been forced to serve as a financial minister under the rebel durbar, but old age and timidity soon unfitted him for office, and hastened his death.

The kotwal, or city magistrate, was one Ally Reiza Beg, son of the late Museeta Beg, a famous kotwal of Lucknow.

Ally Reiza Beg was made extra assistant commissioner in Oude on annexation. During the siege of the Residency he wrote a petition to Sir James

Outram, G.C.B., in which he stated that he was nominated by the rebels to be kotwal of the city, and was obliged to accept it. The appointment is a very lucrative one.

Rajah Dhunput Rae, son of Rajah Oolputt Rae, was the paymaster-general, enjoying a salary of one hundred and fifty rupees a month. The state of this pay office may be conceived when the fact is appreciated that the accounts of this office had never once been settled since the Oude dynasty was established. Owing to the extensive and intricate nature of the frauds prevailing all through the department, the "pay office" had become a proverb, and the expression "Is it the pay office, that it cannot be settled?" was commonly used as the *ultima Thule* short of which all things were possible. No Asiatic Hercules arose to cleanse this Augean stable; and as a *dernier ressort*, the office was actually given out on contract; after this, the attempts of regiments and officials to realize anyhow the pay due to them, may almost be pardoned, and at the same time it ceases to be a matter of surprise that subordinates thus cheated by their superiors out of probably two-thirds of their salary should still cling fondly to the government which cheated them, when we remember how very generally those cheated officials repaid themselves by extortions double and treble the amount defrauded from them, and therefore naturally hugged the system which provided a plea for extortion to those who had consciences, and opened a wide field of enterprise to the clever and avaricious who had none.

One more character in the Oude administration must be noticed, namely, the assistant to the minister. This assistant, a Mahomedan convert from Hindooism, was styled in Oude Shurfoodowlah Gholam Ruza, but was better known by the somewhat homely one of Juggurnauth Bunnea. Gholam Ruza was the name given on conversion; "Shurfoodowlah" was the title given to him subsequently by the king, Umjud Ally Shah, when he deprived his minister, Shurfoodowlah, of office. The title was given to the Bunnea to add to the disgrace of the former minister. He had great influence over the new minister, and, by his unceasing diligence, combined with great natural talent, though he could neither read nor write Persian, contrived to unite in himself a very numerous string of offices, amongst which the following were not the least profitable:—The hozoor tuhseel, or office into which more especially direct revenue payments were made by those who held that privilege; the payment of all begums and wives of sorts; the supplying all khilluts, or presents, ordered by the king for presentation; the contract of all city bazaars, town duties, prostitutes, and public buildings.

It may be conceived that there was no feasting in the house of Juggurnauth Bunnea on the day of annexation; but with the amiable versatility of his class he at once obeyed his king's behests, determinedly refrained from offering armed opposition to the new government, and tendered his submission. In due time, probably only for the sake of his family, he sought and obtained, under the British rule, extensive city contracts, which, however, but faintly resembled the former comfortable annuities.

Having passed down the lists of influential men around the king, forming, if we may so denominate the heterogeneous mass, his government in the capital, there remains, to complete this slight review of the Oude government, the consideration of the system of government in the provinces, which, radiating from such a centre, bore many of its most striking characteristics.

Oude was divided into twenty-two chuckladarrees, or districts, including nizamuts, chuckladarree, hozoor tuhseel, the revenues of which were given out on contract, and the contractors for which were styled chuckladars. A nâzim was superior to a chuckladar, and was entitled to a salute of from seven to eleven guns whilst marching; latterly, as the fair sex exerted its influence, one of these chuckladarships was held by a female under the title of chuckladarnee, or darogah of the "chucklah," the place where prostitutes congregate: her *name* was Hydree, a prostitute; she held the contract of the revenue on prostitution in the city of Lucknow; it amounted to fifty thousand rupees per annum.

Chuckladars were of two kinds: 1st. The lakalamee chuckladar, or one that was under obligation to pay a fixed sum per annum; he received *no* pay or salary. 2nd. The amanee chuckladar, or one that paid into the treasury whatever he could collect; he received a fixed salary.

A chuckladar could inflict any punishment short of taking life; but, as all his sentences of imprisonment were carried out at Lucknow, it was no common occurrence for a prisoner sent in, under sentence of imprisonment for life, by some chuckladar, to be at large within a short period, and entering on a new career, which, by the peculiar nature of Asiatic advancement, might end ere long in the life prisoner being a rival chuckladar.

It is necessary to understand clearly the important

position of these farmers of the revenue, who held almost uncontrolled sway over the great mass of the people beyond the confines of the capital itself. They scattered over their districts subordinate agents, corresponding to our tuhseeldars and thanadars, giving them each a small body guard from the class of mercenary soldiers called nujjeebs. When these subordinate collectors were unable to extort the often exorbitant sum demanded as revenue, the chuckladar called in and received the aid of the king's troops to coerce the unfortunate victims.

This arrangement had, however, its own little difficulties and drawbacks, for it was necessary to reward those king's troops for doing their duty, though nominally they were at the chuckladar's disposal to use as he pleased.

At all times it was the custom for the chuckladars to pay all officers of regiments exactly the same sum as that which they were supposed and did sometimes receive monthly from the king's treasury; this apparently doubled their pay, though it was probably the only stipend they received regularly. The troops also came in for their share of consideration from the chuckladar.

It sometimes happened that regiments ten months in arrears, and out on district duty with chuckladars, mutinied, and put their own officers into confinement until the government awoke to the necessity of paying them. An order for payment on the chuckladar of the district they were in generally followed this move; and as it was not improbable that at the same time the zemindars had forgot to pay up all the revenue demand on them, and the chuckladar forgot to remit to Lucknow any amount those zemindars possibly had remembered and paid, this sudden order for payment on the chuckladars was extremely awkward.

From these irregularities it must not be imagined that any of the parties concerned had the slightest desire to be relieved; all were alike fascinated by the arrangement being delightfully uncertain. The chuckladar and sepoy were content in the chance of extortion, and the zemindar with evading the just demand on himself by some less fortunate victim having to pay double.

A curious system, however, arose from this state of affairs, called the "*kubz*." The commanding officer of the troops comes forward and stands security to the king for as much of the revenue as he can get entrusted to him to collect, often three or four times more than is required to pay his men all their arrears. It is a speculation into which the men heartily enter, always getting their officer to stand security for as large a sum as possible. The officer was entitled to five per cent. on all the money he collected, besides nuzzurs, or presents, he received on taking this contract, or *kubz.*

His men were at once spread out in dustuks, or billeted wherever revenue was not paid up at once; for instance, a forgetful zemindar would have one or more sepoys billeted on him, to whom he must pay a daily sum, fixed according to his means, until he remembers to pay up the revenue in full to the commanding officer. Half of this daily tax the sepoy considered the right of his officer, who had assumed the responsibility of the contract, and faithfully gave it up to him.

By this arrangement the troops effectually secured to themselves their pay, and any slight additions they could pick up; the larger the sum to be collected, the more chances for all parties. Many native commanders succeeded in obtaining from victims absolutely unable to pay, probably from prior extortions of the chuckladar, bonds on the land, by which they were eventually able to eject the original landholder and take possession.

This *kubz* could be carried on in another mode, and was done so by the cavalry and artillery commandants, who would themselves remain in Lucknow sending out on contract their men and guns for the collecting of revenue; the contractor went with the troops, and they took care he paid them out of the collections all arrears due to them; whilst the commandants, it may be presumed, did not find themselves forgotten.

From the foregoing remarks it will be readily understood how justice in the land was at a discount, and what little justice a chuckladar, even if he desired it, could effect, when remission from punishments awarded by him could be readily purchased in Lucknow. The same perversion of justice extended through all the land interests, and the chuckladar could give mouwafie lands, or nankar, in perpetuity; this is the payment of a small yearly sum, which remains fixed for ever, and on payment of it, and no more, the land remains free of all demands.

It is, I believe, giving but a correct idea of this system to say that a chuckladar was a speculator, whose sole object was to get as cheap a contract as he could, and repay himself by extortion from the people, carried to the utmost extent possible. But there is a limit even to extortion, and the annals of Oude furnish many episodes replete with tragedies, natural results of such a system.

Allusion has been made to the army, which upheld this objectionable system, and its paternity, the government, but some further notice of it is desirable.

The army was composed as follows: nineteen (19) regular regiments clothed and drilled according to European style; of these five were commanded by European officers in the king of Oude's service: each regiment averaged 800 men; thirty-two irregular regiments, or nujjeebs, each regiment averaging 500 men.

Each of the regiments commanded by European officers had a battery attached to it of six (6) guns, thus:—one 8-inch mortar; one 8-inch howitzer; two 18-pounders; two 9-pounders. Probably the king had about 1,000 guns or more, besides these, of all sorts and sizes.

Cavalry.—Irregular cavalry, nine regiments, each regiment averaging 450 men; one regiment in the uniform of our regular cavalry, numbering 300, and were without horses; two regiments of regular cavalry, composed of African troopers, and numbering 400 to 600 each; four regiments of regular cavalry of about 400 each; and camel riders with the zumbooruck, or large gun, about 300.

It was said that the king of Oude's army, including

all ranks and servants, classes, sweepers, bildars, bheestees, &c., amounted to 50,000 men.

The principal duties of the army consisted in quelling internal disturbances, collecting revenue by aiding nazims, chuckladars, &c., in coercing refractory zemindars, and in furnishing guards for the cities, towns, ferries, &c., of Oude.

The pay was nominally five rupees per month to sepoys in regular regiments, and from three rupees eight annas to four rupees per month to those in the Nujjeeb irregular regiments.

The regular cavalry troopers received nine rupees per month; the irregular troopers, who furnished their own horses and equipment, received nineteen rupees per month. Each horse in the irregular cavalry was stamped with a Persian letter, and a stamp tax of nominally five rupees per horse (in reality much more) was levied at Lucknow.

The artillery, whether attached to regular regiments or otherwise, received seven rupees per month.

The various nazims and chuckladars had numerous armed retainers, styled "sebundees," entertained generally for the Fusselee year, or season of cultivation, from October to October. These men were employed in thanahs, or police stations, and in assisting the regular troops in their several duties, especially

2

in collecting revenue. Sebundee is derived from *sepah*, soldier; *Hindee*, of India.

It will be well now to notice the people and their chiefs on whom this government, this army, so heavily sat, and from whom they drew those vast sums of which, had but a fair share been spent on the country that supplied them, the province of Oude would have been second to none in agriculture and commerce.

Her splendid soil always responded richly to the hasty and irregular labour of the often necessarily armed ploughman, and her command of river communication always insured markets for her produce.

But it was far otherwise; the fruit of the peasant's toil was sent to the capital, there to be lavishly squandered by a wanton king and his degraded associates.

The result was that Lucknow, the capital, became the residence of an enormous class of parasites, who were fed by such a system, and whose powers of reproduction filled every grade of society, from the court favourite down to the Lucknow "shoda;" there reproduction ceased,—human reason could be connected with no lower nature.

The capital at the time of annexation contained 700,000 inhabitants; an assemblage of human beings who were principally, no doubt, accumulated year by year to supply the wants of the court and its countless hangers on, as the revenues of the country through successive reigns were more and more expended in the capital. It is impossible to enumerate all the parties which constituted that very large proportion of the city population whose livelihood was derived solely from the court and its dependants; suffice it to say, they were exceedingly numerous and, for the most part, utterly worthless. Accustomed to a life of nearly complete ease, or at best but fitful labour, the annexation to them brought but the choice of labour or starvation, and was indeed a day of mourning.

The character of such miserable creatures, such overgrowths of a diseased state of society, may not be taken as bearing the slightest resemblance to that of the veritable people of Oude.

The province supplied soldiers largely, not only to the Bengal army but to Bombay and Central India. Her population, nurtured amidst constant petty turmoil and bloodshed, succeeded in carrying on agriculture and commerce to a far greater degree than could have been expected, and under circumstances which would have depopulated most provinces.

Still the small zemindar, or landholder, and the

labourer who tilled the soil, and who often ploughed girt with his sword and shield, were, under the old *régime*, most depressed, most ill-treated.

Too weak to resist, lowest in the scale of extortion, the small land cultivator rarely retained of the fruits of his labour more than sufficient to support Indian life; and the only wages he could afford to those who shared with him this manual toil was, in Oude, usually three and a half seers of bajra (a very common grain) per diem, equal to about 6 lbs. weight English measure. Passing in a direct line from Lucknow to Shahjehanpore, in September, 1856, I went through many tracts where the old state of things remained untouched, and where men and children, leaving the plough, ran to catch a glimpse of one of that foreign race of whom they had often heard, but had never seen, and under whose rule they had lately but most vaguely heard they soon would come. In their simple mind the news of the annexation raised but one new train of thought,—what share shall I now retain of the fruits of my toil? will this new master take less than my old one? He could not more; to me therefore it may be good.

To such men a change of masters was objectionable or otherwise, simply as it affected their own life interests. They had no nationality, and had been too long depressed ever to combine and lift a finger to aid either the good or the bad master. No doubt these petty landholders welcomed the annexation; very soon they saw a real chance of reaping a fair share of what they sowed, and they were not backward to declare their satisfaction. Many voluntary expressions of pleasure were daily made to me by such men; nor was it at all wonderful; they could not be worse, and might be better.

In former years the small remnant of their crops that the district lord left them was sadly diminished by the extortions of many smaller lords; and even the very Passee cattle grazed on their lands untouched. Those Passees, those freebooters of the jungles, were too great adepts with the bow and arrow for any poor man to drive their cattle away openly, though many a stone was slyly thrown at the unwitting beasts.

I witnessed this myself, but the dread of the silent arrow was so great that they begged me not to take any notice of them; they would, perhaps, scare the cattle away gradually.

The Passees noticed above are supposed to be an aboriginal race of Hindoos, small in stature, well formed, supple, and sleek; with a quick eye and amazing dexterity with the bow and arrow, he is always a formidable enemy to meet in his native jungles. Their habits are predatory, and they live considerably on the pigs they keep and the game they hunt; possessing the lower characteristics of many savages, they, nevertheless, are proverbially true to trust, and have great bodily courage.

It was very common for bankers of Lucknow, who wished to remit cash to a distance, to collect as many Passees as were necessary, give them 100 rupees, with directions to deliver it to a certain man in a certain place. Each Passee started off, taking his own road, and faithfully deposited the money, receiving as a reward, if the distance was about sixty miles, probably two rupees.

Like all mercenaries, they fight for those who pay them best, and readily change sides, according to circumstances.

In villages they usually lived apart—a little community, and did all the duties of chokeedars and guides. Vast numbers of their brethren adhered to their old haunts, the jungles, and carried on most extensive fairs of stolen cattle; the only precaution necessary to avoid future trouble, being to sell an animal stolen in the south to a purchaser from the north, and on this point they seldom deceived their regular customers. As a race, they are anything but beneficial to Oude.

The sweeping away of those jungles which act as nurseries for vagabonds of all sorts, will do much towards ameliorating their condition, by forcing them to seek a livelihood in some of the ordinary channels of civilization. In warfare the natives invariably employ these men, and often as miners, at which work they are clever and indefatigable. They attested this by a remarkable robbery, effected prior to the mutiny, when, by means of a mine of immense length dug by these Passees, the thieves got completely under the treasury of a begum and removed a great amount of valuable property.

Subsequently these Passees have figured in the mutiny as plunderers and mercenaries; during the siege of Lucknow many of the enemy's mines were made by them, and their dexterity and perseverance principally entailed on the garrison that incessant labour which was necessary to destroy, by countermines, the perpetual efforts of these wretches: four of the enemy's miners whom we suffocated by an explosion, and dug out, were all Passees.

It is unnecessary to notice the class of middlemen between the wealthy talookdar or zemindar, and those lowest in the scale which we have now briefly touched on. Once the means of subsistence were secured, unfettered by any wholesome dread of law or certain retribution, they emulated their superiors in oppression, and sought by all means, fair or foul, to aggrandize themselves and families: with no powers of combination, they were not individually powerful enough to be of much value as friend or foe to any government.

Not so the large talookdar or zemindar: they were a class which, formidable to any government, were constantly at war with their own. Ever stirring to increase their power, they hesitated not to avail themselves, by armed force, of all those chances which an Asiatic government, lost in licentiousness, offered to the daring and unscrupulous; less exacting than the chuckladars, they treated their own tenants with some degree of consideration, but all else were lawful prey. To dispossess a small but ancient landholder, whose lands lay temptingly near, was an ordinary occurrence, in which but two parties took much interest, the possessor and the dispossessed. It is very probable that the village thus forcibly transferred may have fared actually better under its new and rich suzerain than under its old, but poor one. The rich lord could well make large advances for village improvements, wells, &c., and often did so, in addition to the necessary advances for the annual seed crops and other agricultural purposes; whereas the poor man could but with difficulty probably borrow the necessary advances for sowing from some close-fisted bunnea, who found such men safe investments—comfortable annuities; it is probable, therefore, that the village benefited by being owned by a richer lord, and would make but small demur, if any, to the transfer. Thus passed away lands, houses, and ancient tenements, many of which boasted, and could show, title-deeds bearing the seal and superscription of the emperors of the Delhi Empire in its best days. These interesting deeds were, many of them, extant in Oude at the annexation: I saw several, and doubtless they will be again forthcoming when the rights of land come under consideration.

The revenues of Oude may be taken as aggregating rupees 12,98,449 in the year Fusselee 1263, nominally; in reality, one crore, or about 100 lacs.

The brief sketch of Oude, her king, court, and officials, with the system of government prevailing in her capital and districts, and the treatment of the various classes of men composing her population, will probably assist in forming a correct opinion as to the reception our annexation would meet with from Oude so constituted. A further short notice of Oude after the annexation, showing our system and its effects, will give a sufficient basis from which to understand clearly with what spirit the men of Oude would meet the mutiny of the Bengal army in 1857.

Simultaneous with the annexation and the submission of the king, followed by that of his people in obedience to his written orders, there was spread over the length and breadth of Oude a government, modelled on the Punjaub system, complete in all its European and native officials, and supported by an army of 20,600 men, as follows:—

Artillery Regiment	12 Guns.	
„ Local	18 „	
Cavalry Regiments		600 Sabres.
Irregular ditto		600 „
Locals		1,500 „
Police		700 „
Infantry Regiments		6,000 „
„ Locals		8,000 „
„ Police		2,400 „
„ Europeans		800 „
Total		20,600 „

Artillery	30 Guns.
Cavalry	3,400
Infantry	17,200—

800 men of which were Europeans.

The task of this army was easy, simply occupation of the country; but that of the administration, arduous and difficult in the extreme.

The actions of men, to whom from the first dawn of manhood law had existed only to be opposed, and with whom justice was a tradition, had now to be judged by a system which, while it aimed at impartial justice to all, yet knew no opposition to its edicts, no mitigation of its sentences. The fiat of the district judge could no longer be evaded by a purchased remission from the capital, and blood spilt in the village fray must now be redeemed by years of arduous toil in chains.

The institution of inquiries into rights of property synchronous with the settlements for revenue, and involving the consideration of the actions and writings, not only of the present, but of past generations, unavoidably increased the difficulties already felt in making those settlements; there being but few instances where the time was fitting or sufficiently ample to make that thorough investigation, without which any just result from such inquiries was impossible.

To show how difficult it was for the English assistant commissioner to convince himself who was the man with whom he should in justice make the revenue settlement, I will mention a case of very common occurrence. I state this on the information of an Oude officer, who settled a considerable district himself.

Going back some hundred years, suppose the owner of an estate or the talookdar finds it troublesome to collect the revenue from all his tenants, he looks round amongst his friends, selects one man in whom he has confidence, and to whom he gives the farming of his revenue on contract; this arrangement being simply that the agent pays a regular fixed annual sum to the owner, and then collects the revenue himself.

It is not necessary here to inquire how the talookdar got hold of the estate; suffice it to say, that a hundred years ago he was in possession.

In the course of time this talookdar dies, and his son, we will suppose, renews his father's contract with the old contractor; when this latter also dies, we will suppose, as was often the case, that the contract is renewed with the contractor's son, and thus runs on from father to son in one family talookdaree right, and in the other family the right of collection. At last an exacting and powerful chuckladar arrives, and the talookdar, as unable to resist as he is unwilling to pay, runs away; in many cases this effectually checkmated the chuckladar, who reduced his demands accordingly, but in this instance we will suppose the chuckladar clever, as well as powerful. He immediately gets hold of the contractor's family, and by promising to acknowledge them to be the rightful owners of the soil, induces them to make all the collections as before, and pay him instead of paying the talookdar.

To perfect this, the chuckladar gives regular official government documents to the contractor as if he was the real owner. Now supposing this state of things to run on for some years, we can understand the difficulties attending an investigation in our courts as to who was the right man for the British Government to settle with, and if so, for how much of the land, as the estate might have been very much increased and added to by the contractor after he became acknowledged lord.

On examination, the old contractor's family will show testimony, oral and written, to eighty years back, that they always collected the revenue, whilst no proof of their being mere agents comes up at all; and to crown all, he triumphantly shows the settlements signed by the last chuckladar with him, as lord of the soil. It is easy to state that all former chuckladarree records were destroyed by such and such a disturbance, so common in Oude, if any attempt was made to get hold of them for reference.

The people generally know who is the real lord of the soil, though all do not, if the contractor has farmed the revenue for many years; but natives will not speak just when they are wanted.

It is not difficult to perceive how perfectly unavoidably many men were put into possession, and many put out of possession, of villages and lands, possibly very unjustly: all would, no doubt, have soon been rectified as further inquiries proceeded, but *pro tem.* numbers smarted, and those numbers were not the least powerful in Oude. Probably sufficient data have now been shown regarding the people of Oude, from which to gather a very fair conception of how our rule was appreciated by them, and in what spirit they would enter on the new field of chances opened to them by the mutiny of 1857.

When first our rule was established, the inhabitants, ordered to submit by their own sovereign, received the annexation without any very manifest dislike. Of course I exclude here those parasites and attendants on the court, who were but the excrescences of a system, and no index to the feelings of the people.

The poorest cultivators and small zemindars received with joy a system which they knew from the reports of the neighbouring districts under our rule, always benefited them; and it may be fairly assumed, that these classes of men have throughout the late disturbances longed for the return of our rule, though it never will occur to them that they could either individually or collectively aid us: at the same time, there is no doubt many of them have obeyed lately the re-established rule of their old masters, and perforce borne arms against us. That large mercantile class, amongst whom the grain merchants or bunneas form a considerable portion, ought to prefer any rule which secures to them an unmolested enjoyment of their much-loved gains; but by no sign, act, or word, did this class, during the disturbances, show they at all appreciated our rule which fostered them; not one tittle of their vast wealth did they offer towards the restoration of order, nor did they visibly exercise, for the suppression of the rebellion, that influence which the holders of great wealth invariably possess. Probably no race amongst men live so entirely for themselves. Never contributing one iota to the revenue, they often tend very considerably to injure it by lending money on lands at such an exorbitant interest, that both the cultivator and the land are soon in the market,—both alike ruined.

The apathy of the ignorant cultivator can be explained; the active resistance of the dispossessed talookdar understood; but to what cause are we to attribute that apathy of these traders, who, knowing the value of an equitable rule, will not stir one finger to procure it?

* * * * * *

Lastly, the large landholders and talookdars, with other wealthy men of Oude, not connected with the court, finding, at the first outset of annexation, that they were not to fight, looked on with almost content at the commencement of our system: they but half understood our courts, and had not yet felt them.

Soon, however, as disagreeable inquiries arose about their landed rights, each felt the enemy, and, like the hedgehog, curled up accordingly. All were not equally dissatisfied; many were left in undisturbed possession of their estates, but unavoidably and justly were called on to pay up those arrears of revenue which were due from them to the former administration. This they disliked and endeavoured to evade by every species of chicanery and procrastination. It followed, as a matter of course, that non-payment of revenue met with the usual treatment in our courts, and the lands were taken from the defaulter. Other wealthy men, again, who did not owe any arrears to the late government still suffered from the faulty nature of their landed rights, losing many villages they had lately and forcibly seized *vi et armis*; and, shorn of half their power, they saw with no kindly feelings, villages and lands return to the poor but rightful owners, to eject whom had probably cost them the blood of their best friends.

From the foregoing sketch it may be readily understood that, from the very constitution of the various ranks of life in Oude, combined with events occurring after the annexation, all were, at the first burst of the mutiny, inclined either for active enmity or passive friendship; and that the European community could expect no assistance from the people in crushing the spirit of the mutiny, or stemming the current of rebellion.

Such was the attitude of the people of Oude, as the year 1857 unfolded its pages. The first act of defiance open and determined against the British rule in Oude, proceeding apparently from religious motives, and, therefore, in unison with the rumours of the time, was that of a moulvie, or Mahomedan priest at Fyzabad, who, giving himself out, as usual, to be a real descendant of the Prophet, entered the city in some degree of state, with horses, camels, and armed followers, the whole locating themselves in the public serai, or resting house for travellers. This moulvie, there known as Ahmed Alee Shah, was a native of Arcot, in the Madras Presidency, understood English very tolerably, and was possessed of considerable acumen and boldness. He failed to excite that religious fervour in others which burnt so fiercely in himself, and by which he hoped to envenom all. A Soonee himself, he but little interested the great majority of the Mahomedans there, who were Sheahs, and he produced no effect at all on the far larger mass of the population who were Hindoos. These latter had yet fresh in their recollection the bitter rage and hate of those Mahomedans who had very lately, under the old rule, fought desperately to dispossess them of their temple, the "Hunooman Ghurree." An idle legend that a Mahomedan saint was, in centuries back, buried beneath this Hindoo sanctuary of the monkey god, was the cause of a most vicious attack on it by a set of fanatical Mahomedans, which, though it ended in their most complete slaughter, yet cost the life of many a Hindoo brave.

To return to the moulvie: this man, after passing through a vast number of cities and stations under our rule, in all parts of India, and establishing his disciples therein, reached Fyzabad in February, 1857. Subsequent investigation elicited that everywhere he had preached a jehad, or religious war against the Kafirs, or infidels, as the Europeans were politely designated. From some places he had been summarily ejected, but in others evaded expulsion, meeting with no real check until he came to Fyzabad. Here, after preaching undisturbed, apparently for two or three days, a chuprassee informed the magistrate of the really dangerous tendency of this man's doings, and, accordingly, the officer in charge of the city issued the necessary orders for his arrest. The principal terms demanded from this moulvie were, that he and his armed followers, numbering about seven, should give up their arms, which should be kept in safe custody so long as they remained in the city, and returned to them on their departure; further, that all this preaching, this distribution of money, so conducive to disturbance of the public peace, should be entirely put an end to. A deliberate refusal was given to every demand, and armed resistance threatened to every attempt at coercion, either on the part of the magistrate and city officer or their native officials. An infantry guard was necessarily put on the moulvie and his men during the night, and, early the next morning, an infantry company, after failing at surprising them, attacked them *vi et armis.* Maddened by exciting drugs, these fanatics fought fiercely. The young European officer, Ensign Thomas, of the 22nd Native Infantry, escaping a fatal blow, received a slight cut on the head; several sepoys received severe cuts, and it was some minutes before all were shot down but the moulvie and two men. These latter were finally captured, faint from loss of blood; and the moulvie, wounded in the shoulder, was induced to come out of a dark corner in which he sought shelter, by the promise of a fair trial if he gave up his arms, or instant death if he refused.

He and his men were eventually confined under a guard in cantonments, as he seemed too dangerous a character to keep in the city gaol. I was at Fyzabad at this time, and did not observe that the manners or attitude of the people towards Europeans was in the slightest degree altered by this transaction. Officers were constantly passing and repassing through the city. It would have been easy to detect any sympathy on the part of the people with the imprisoned moulvie. Fyzabad, no doubt, was then a loyal city, and remained so until the mutineers, hunting for British officers through its streets, convinced the people that our rule had indeed passed away. The whole country from Fyzabad to Lucknow, which I reached on the 12th of March, presented the same aspect of peace and quiet which I had observed, whilst marching, in the previous month, from Bairam Ghaut to Fyzabad along the banks of the Ghogra River.

In March, 1857, the reins of government in Oude were assumed by the late Sir Henry Lawrence, K.C.B. The early rumblings of the earthquake, felt first at Berhampore and Barrackpore, were soon heard all over India, and found Oude still in that transition state from anarchy to order, on which all popular commotions act violently and with electric rapidity.

That remarkable and still unexplained passage through Oude and elsewhere of the "Chupattee" symbol, occurred early in 1857, and, from the first movement of its advent into Oude, spread with such amazing rapidity, that it was calculated ten days more than sufficed for every village chowkedar in Oude to have received the little bread-cake, and made and passed on similar little bread-cakes to every village chowkedar within the ordinary radius of his travels.

The natives generally may have viewed this sign manual flying through their villages,—so common a method amongst men in the early stages of civilization to warn all, for either peace or war,—as a forerunner of some universal popular outbreak, but by whom, or with what class, the standard of rebellion would be raised, certainly was not generally known.

The army, murmuring against the introduction of a new sort of cartridge, so rapidly echoed by all our military stations, may have pointed some men's minds towards the army as the brand which *was* smouldering and would soon burst into flame; but the mass of the people, little anticipating so extensive a mutiny, comprehended but slowly the vastness of its effects. To the inhabitants of Oude, it was no unusual occurrence for the government to be at armed variance with its own troops; the elasticity of an Asiatic government fully admitted of a very serious mutiny, followed by a most degrading compromise, on its part, without the government very materially suffering; hence, undoubtedly, at the commencement, our new subjects here did not look upon the first buddings of the poisonous weed as anything very unusual, very serions. The unnatural plant had flourished amidst their homesteads for many a long year, nourished by the blood of constant strife; and it is not a little probable, that the very large element in our late Bengal army, supplied from this nursery of our native armies, as

Oude is aptly designated, owed in a very considerable degree to its early education, amidst scenes of violence and oppression, that fitness, that readiness for mutiny and bloodshed which wanted but a spark to light it, and which, once burning, soon ignited the less inflammable zemindarry matter around it.

The friends and relations of such men, and the inhabitants of Oude generally, no doubt, believed that, as heretofore, the soldiers would get what they wanted and that events would soon settle down; but still each individual instinctively girded up his loins, lest he should lose the chance of despoiling others, or be despoiled himself.

Events and wonderful tales thickened somewhat rapidly in March and April. Rumours of the hostile intentions of the British Government towards the religion of their Mahomedan and Hindoo subjects were in rapid circulation. Cartridges greased with the fat of pigs for Mahomedans, and of cows for Hindoos, were stated to be in preparation by thousands, and the mixing pounded bones with the (*atta*) flour, were amongst the many absurd reports which as soon found their way into Oude as into other parts of India. Events seemed pointing to a war of caste or religion, the former so prized by the Hindoos, the latter by the Mahomedans.

It is impossible to mention here all the various

steps taken by the late lamented Sir Henry Lawrence, K.C.B., to preserve the soldiery in their duty and the people in their allegiance. Every conciliatory measure was adopted, consistent with the dignity of the British Government; and there is no doubt that, by his untiring energy, discretion, ability, and determination, he *did* fan into a flame for a while the wavering loyalty of many of the native officers and men, and that the army and people generally felt that his was a firm and an experienced hand. In spite of the numerous tamperers with our sepoys, no open demonstration was ventured on, either by the army or the people, during the months of March and April. The Mahomedan fanatic preached his religious war in holes and corners, though the Hindoo pundit more openly prophesied the English reign was over, a new era had commenced; but as yet the arm of the law smothered the serpent's hissing, and cauterized the spreading sore by numerous arrests followed by executions.

These arrests very forcibly showed how much good still remained in the army. Plotters, tamperers, and preachers were alike seized, and often on the information of native officers and soldiers, who aided in the arrest of the offenders. It may be naturally supposed that such loyalty under such circumstances was rewarded with an open hand; but will it be credited, that, with few exceptions, all thus loyal equally joined the mutineers, and that one native officer who had received a handsome present for conspicuous loyalty, was hanged for as conspicuous mutiny six weeks afterwards: the motives that sway an Asiatic mind set all ordinary reasoning at defiance.

It may convey a correcter idea of the difficulties to be overcome by the Government, and the danger threatening the European community, if the strength of the military force in the capital is here mentioned.

Military force in the capital and its environs on April 30th, 1857,—

Native Infantry,		3 Regiments,	13th, 48th, 71st.
"	Irregular ditto,	2 "	4th, 7th.
"	Police ditto	1 "	3rd.
"	Cavalry, 7th Light Cavalry.		
"	Mounted Police, 1½ Regiment.		
"	Irregular Oude,	1 "	2nd.
"	Artillery, 2 Batteries.		

This, taking a native infantry regiment at 800 men, and a native cavalry corps at 600, gives as follows:—

Native Infantry	Regulars . . .	2,400	
" "	Irregulars . .	1,600	
" "	Police . . .	800	
			4,800
Native Cavalry,	Regular . . .	600	
" "	Irregular . . .	600	
" "	Mounted Police . .	900	
			2,100
"	Artillery, two batteries.		
Europeans—H. M.'s 32nd, strength . .			700
Artillery, one weak Company.			

In the very city itself, all this force was not then congregated. In cantonments, three miles from the city, the one regiment of regular cavalry and three regiments of regular infantry with the artillery were located; all else was in the city. The cantonments were connected by a good pucka road with the city, which crossed the iron bridge, and about midway between the Residency and the Muchee Bhawun, a fort so called. This iron bridge, with the stone bridge, formed the sole permanent communication over the river Goomtee for the accommodation of the inhabitants on either bank.

A bridge of boats considerably lower down the river, but liable to all the accidents of such a bridge, was maintained, and formed the only communication across the river below the Residency.

Sir Henry Lawrence, K.C.B., had from the first felt the hopelessness of resisting the mutiny of the regular army by the aid of the irregular Oude locals, horse and foot; these regiments were many of them old king's regiments, which had been transferred *en masse*, officers and men, into our employ at a rate of pay considerably below that enjoyed by our regular army.

Sir Henry, therefore, foreseeing that the mutiny, if it rolled on unstayed, would as soon absorb in its rapid accumulating wave, the irregular as the regular mercenary in our service, entered energetically on that line of proceedings which, staying the wave to the utmost, caused it eventually to break around the defences of the "Baillie Guard."

Thus far, to the end of April, though an unnatural excitement prevailed everywhere, yet no open mutiny had occurred; times were exciting enough—they were soon to be more so.

On the 30th April, the 7th Regiment of Oude Irregular Infantry manifested, amongst its recruits; who had commenced ball-cartridge practice about the middle of the month, a reluctance to use the cartridge. The officer then in the lines, Lieutenant Mecham, and from whom the account of this incident is taken, at once pointed out to the men the absurdity of raising objections to using that, which they well knew and admitted was the usual cartridge, and which moreover they had been using for the last fifteen days. The men appeared satisfied, and at the moment no more was thought of it; the drill proceeded on that day as usual. On the 1st of May, however, the sergeant-major again reported that there was a steady refusal on the part of the recruits to bite the cartridge, and many had refused either to receive or handle them. The whole squad, about thirty men, were confined in the quarter-guard, and the native officers were peremptorily ordered to disperse the remaining recruits, who, after their drill, had refused to break off, and had remained assembled in gangs in the lines. The native officers generally appeared reluctant to interfere, and seemed disinclined to offer any assistance; but the havildar major, who throughout the mutiny behaved most creditably, informed Lieut. Mecham that the recruits had been taunted by the old sepoys with having lost caste by using the cartridges.

It is seen here that "caste" produced in the Hindoo that spirit of mutiny which in the Mahomedan is traced to religion.

The native officers were shortly assembled by the commanding officer, Lieutenant Watson, and clearly shown the impropriety of their conduct; but, the result remaining unsatisfactory, it was determined to report the event to superior authority on the next morning. However, on that morning, May 1st, the native officers came up and begged the report to be delayed until, before the assembled regiment on parade, they, the native officers, had bitten the cartridge themselves, when they felt sure all the sepoys would follow their example.

The protestations of the native officers were so

earnest that a parade was ordered, but before the officers could reach it, when ready, the native officers returned and warned the officers against going near the men, who had threatened to shoot any one who attempted to coerce them into using the cartridges, and that the native officers who attempted to fulfil their promise would assuredly be shot. A report was made of this to Brigadier Gray, commanding, who with his staff came to the regiment, and on parade endeavoured to induce them to return to their duty. The men were sullen and the expostulation unavailing; Sir Henry Lawrence was therefore informed of the state of the regiment.

All that night and the next morning the men maintained the same mutinous aspect, some noisy, some sullen; but in the morning, about ten A.M., on the 3rd May, the quartermaster-sergeant came in hastily, and said the men were openly threatening to kill all the European officers; shortly afterwards an unusual commotion was apparent in the lines, the men rushed to the bells of arms, took their arms, and seized the magazine; at the same time the havildar major and a few faithful sepoys came over to the officers and intreated them to escape, as the men had determined to take their lives. The officers armed themselves and went outside, whence they saw the men of the regiment assembled in masses outside their lines, but not showing any apparent intention of advancing on the officers. Seeing this, the officers went towards them, determined to try if any further appeal to their senses could induce them to return to their duty and allegiance. The native commissioned officers came to meet their officers, and assured them no harm should befall them.

After some time, the sepoys so far listened to their officers, that they dispersed and went to their lines, but insisted on retaining their arms. That evening Captain Boileau, of the 2nd Oude Irregular Infantry, and Captain Hardinge, of the 3rd Oude Irregular Cavalry, arrived by order of the Chief Commissioner; the corps was paraded and each company to the question, "Will you bite the cartridge?" replied, "Yes," though their manner was insolent and sullen; no doubt the knowledge of a considerable force then coming from cantonments overawed them at the time. On the arrival of this force, the men were paraded and wheeled into line, the guns of the cantonment being loaded and portfires lighted. A panic seized some of the men, who fled, when the rest grounded arms according to order; nearly all who fled came back on the assurance that violence would not be used to the obedient, and that night the arms of the entire regiment were conveyed to the magazine, and Captain Gall, with the 1st Regiment of Irregular Cavalry, left in camp close to the lines. The next day numbers of the ringleaders were seized, and a court of inquiry eventually elicited that treasonable correspondence had been going on for some time between this regiment and the 48th Native Infantry, then in cantonments, for the object of arranging a mutual rising.

About this time the news of the Delhi mutiny arrived, and Sir Henry Lawrence went to the Moosa Bâgh, where this regiment was cantoned, and, after dismissing almost all the native officers and a number of the non-commissioned officers and men, gave the rest their arms, and they were that day marched down to the city and put into the Dowlutkhânâ. The remainder, thus armed, continued faithful and did good service up to the first day of the siege, when the native officers said the men could stand by us no longer. Sir Henry Lawrence, to meet the wants of a hungry multitude, at the same time enrolled 3,000 police, which, under the vigorous and firm rule of Major Carnegie, the city magistrate, did excellent service. During this month of May, active preparations were going on according to the orders of Sir Henry Lawrence, in collecting grain and provisions for store, and fortifying the fort, called the Muchee Bhawun, an important point in the city to hold.

The deputy commissioner, Mr. Martin, assisted by Mr. Williams, an *extra* assistant commissioner, also Major Carnegie, the city magistrate, and Captain James, head of the commissariat, were all most actively employed even thus early in collecting a large amount of grain and other supplies. By the orders of Sir Henry Lawrence, a force was sent to Cawnpore about the middle of May, as much to get some troops removed from Lucknow, as to make them of some use to the State; the destination of those troops was to be Futtehghur, it being hoped that they would assist in quelling the rebellious spirit of the inhabitants in the districts north of Futtehghur, wherever the authorities there might require them.

Lieutenant Ashe and his battery was sent to Cawnpore and remained there, whilst Captain Hayes, Lieutenant Barber, Lieutenant Carey, and Mr. Fayrer, a volunteer, went on with Major Gall's Irregular Cavalry and some men of other Oude Irregular Cavalry regiments towards Futtehghur.

From subsequent inquiries, it was ascertained

that, after passing Mynpoorie about the 7th or 8th of June, the Irregular Cavalry determined to murder the officers, and commenced by one of the sowars, a Mahomedan, nearly severing Mr. Fayrer's head from his body, as the unfortunate gentleman was drinking water from a mussuck, which a water carrier, in the usual way, poured into his hand. The blow was struck from behind; a Sikh rissaldar who was in the rear, and from whose mouth I elicited most of the facts here given, on coming up at the time, at once raised up the body; the young man was not quite dead, as the windpipe apparently could not have been severed; he muttered twice, called the doctor, and died. The Sikh placed his body in a buggy, which was following behind, whilst the men moved on. Almost immediately afterwards Captain Hayes was cut down, and Lieutenant Barber, after shooting one man with his revolver and wounding three, two of whom he dismounted with his sword, fell pierced by countless bullets; Lieutenant Carey alone escaped back to Mynpoorie, and was pursued in vain. The bodies of the officers were brought into Mynpoorie by the Sikh rissaldar Shere Singh, who had put Lieutenant Barber's body in the buggy; he managed to get away with two other Sikhs from the detachment, on some pretence or other, and eventually four or five other Sikhs got away; all the rest went to Delhi.

Whilst preparations on an active scale were going on at Lucknow, during this month of May, considerable excitement prevailed in all the out-stations, though nowhere else did the European community attempt to provision any place with the view of making a prolonged resistance.

At Mahumdee, on the 10th of May, I visited Mr. James Thomason, the deputy commissioner at that station, which is on the extreme of the Oude frontier, and only eighteen miles from Shahjehanpore. No immediate danger was on the 10th May anticipated by either Mr. Thomason, or Captain Patrick Orr, his assistant; a company, the 9th Oude Irregular Infantry, Captain Orr's old regiment, had just been sent there by Mr. Christian, the commissioner of Setapore, with a few words of advice regarding retreating into the fort at Mahumdee if need be, but no danger was then at all anticipated. Shahjehanpore, which I had also just left, was equally quiet; the regiment then seemed passive, and the officers one and all treated it most trustfully to the last. The only alarming quarter was Setapore. Mr. Christian from the first foresaw that the mutiny would commence with the

41st, and told Mr. Thomason he might depend on the 9th Oude. I remember, however, distinctly that Mr. Thomason, had his own personal safety alone been concerned, intended going for protection to some neighbouring rajah, whose name now I cannot remember: circumstances eventually prevented this; the influx of fugitives from Shahjehanpore, no doubt, decided for him his line of duty, in which he nobly perished.

From the 13th to the 19th May I marched leisurely through the district down to Setapore, examining, with my assistant, Lieutenant F. W. Birch, a line for a new trunk road which he had surveyed; this took us quite through the heart of the country, until I came to Benigunj, opposite Setapore, whence I went in to stay with Mr. Christian. Nothing could then be quieter than the district there. The Mahomedan town of Peyhannee and other places, likely to rise quickly, were all passive.

From Mr. Christian I ascertained the exact state of affairs at Setapore. Always buoyant and sanguine, he looked hopefully to quell the expected rise of the 41st by the aid of the Oude irregular regiments and irregular levies of his own, and for this he had good ground. The 41st Native Infantry and 9th Oude Irregular Infantry had quarrelled some short time previously so much that the men of the one regiment would not bathe at the same ghaut with men of the other. Mr. Christian told me this himself. Colonel Birch, however, commanding the 41st, fully, and to the last, believed his regiment would not mutiny.

I remained at Setapore until the 25th May, on which day I left it. Mr. Christian had carefully gone over with me his project for defence; we had walked together over all the ground, and considered all points. Undoubtedly, if the irregular troops, the 9th and 10th regiments of Oude Irregular Infantry, and the detachment of Fisher's Irregular Cavalry, had remained faithful, Mr. Christian would have averted the crisis, and probably saved the life of every one there. He was well convinced the 41st would rise, and were only biding their time: he saw no place offering a refuge to the ladies, as Lucknow, he deemed, would have more to do to hold itself than was desirable; he therefore determined to make the bold and daring attempt of playing off one arm of the service against the other, the irregulars against the regulars; the result will be shown in its proper place, as also his excellent arrangements for defence. All was done that human wisdom could foresee, and he fell nobly, working to the last. I carried away with me for submission to Sir Henry Lawrence a scheme by Mr. Christian for removing a portion of the dangerous element, the regular troops, from Lucknow, and turning them to some advantage, or, at any rate, neutralizing their evil propensities, by marching them up through Mr. Christian's district, it being his intention eventually to post them along his northern frontier, and, if need be, use them in checking any turbulence on the part of the inhabitants.

This scheme was laid by me on the 26th May before Sir Henry Lawrence, but was not at once taken up. Lucknow was then in a most excited state: the fortifications of the Residency as well as of the Muchee Bhawun were going on rapidly; Major Anderson, the chief engineer, superintended all the fortifications: the former executed chiefly by the late Captain Fulton, Bengal Engineers, and Lieutenant Anderson, Madras Engineers; the latter by Lieutenant Innis, Bengal Engineers. One incessant stream of store carts conveying grain supplies, munitions of war, &c., lined the principal streets. The utmost energies of the Commissariat Department were taxed by Sir Henry Lawrence, who alone fully appreciated the probability of a prolonged siege.

On the 27th Sir Henry Lawrence determined on

carrying out Mr. Christian's scheme, if only to get rid of some of the regular troops. He appointed me his aide-de-camp, and ordered me to proceed with a column as political officer. The route was to be *via* Sundeela and Sandee up towards Futtehghur, and the troops told off were two troops 7th Light Cavalry, 200 men, two companies 48th Native Infantry, 200 men.

In addition to these, however, I had a personal escort of twenty Sikh troopers from the 1st Regiment Oude Irregular Cavalry, and forty nujjeebs, or irregular mercenaries, men who bring their own arms and receive pay, but no accoutrements or dress; also six sepoys 4th Oude Irregular Infantry. As there were pensioners to be paid at Futtehghur, it was considered a good opportunity for Major Marriott to be escorted so far. He accordingly took command of the troops, but my letter of instructions distinctly stated that the movements of the column rested with me. Sir Henry felt that no fixed route could be laid down for the troops to march by, and therefore, once past Sundeela, he left their direction entirely to me.

On the 28th May this small column marched and reached Mulheeabad, a village fourteen miles from Lucknow, on the road to Sundeela. The officers then with it were, besides Major Marriott, Lieutenant Boulton, commanding cavalry, Lieutenant Martin under him, Captain Burmester, commanding the infantry, with Lieutenant Farquharson under him. Captain Staples joined us at Sundeela, with a quarter-master-sergeant, and then, according to orders, Lieutenant Martin was to have returned; but he wished to stay, and it was unsafe his returning by himself, an escort being impossible. Lieutenant Tulloch, Native Infantry, accompanied me as an assistant political, and Dr. Darby was medical officer in charge.

It should have been mentioned that on the 27th May Captain Weston and Lieutenant Mecham, with an escort of one company of that very 7th Regiment, so lately in mutiny at Moosa Bâgh, went to this same village of Mulheeabad for the purpose of quieting the villagers there in open armed revolt. Zemindars of Oude now began to feel the noxious breath of the mutiny, and were not long in becoming completely affected. Our march through Mulheeabad was watched by armed villagers, and this only fourteen miles from Lucknow, where three months previously they dare not have lifted a finger, and where the year before, in September, I had encamped in perfect security.

Captain Weston and Lieutenant Mecham, when the column before mentioned passed through on the 28th, were in imminent danger, surrounded by an insolent Mahomedan population, to whom everything was a grievance, and from whom Captain Weston could elicit no real tangible cause of rebellion; turbulent spirits, they knew the army would mutiny, and therefore dared to take up arms. The only troops to protect these officers were men the infantry portion of whom had once mutinied a short time before, and the police cavalry, who were doubtful; however, on this occasion, providentially, they were faithful; for had they been treacherous, nothing, humanly speaking, could have saved their lives, and no doubt our column, *en route* for Futtehghur, would at once have followed their example.

At this time affairs in Oude were rapidly approaching a crisis; the troops at the capital ready to rise; the out-stations only waiting for Lucknow to do so, that they might follow their example.

True the native troops in Lucknow were much weakened by the column just sent away, and the authorities were keenly on the alert; but Sir Henry Lawrence appeared to see from the beginning that the mutiny would spread far and wide. He had himself spared no exertions, no means to stay the tide: grand durbars were held, in which the faithful soldiers who brought forward miscreants tampering with the men were rewarded with an open hand, and on those occasions Sir Henry was wont to say a few words of advice to the native nobility, officers and soldiers assembled around him. His words were described by an eye-witness as plainly spoken, with energy and candour. Delicately alluding to the honours which decorated his breast, and those of many native officers present, he reminded them of the fatherly government which had bestowed them, and whose kindness and consideration was as great as its justice was sure and impartial. With all his care and solicitude for the welfare of Lucknow, Sir Henry was not unmindful of the out-stations of Oude: he knew well it was not necessary for him to remind British officers, civil and military, that England expected every man to do his duty; but he issued letters as events thickened, and results were but too palpable to all the officers, civil and military, scattered over the provinces, desiring them to consider they had his permission to provide for their own safety when mutiny and rebellion became inevitable, and not to wait for its actual burst into violence. With equal forethought he telegraphed to Allahabad, warning the authorities against trusting the fort in the hands of the Sikhs. So long as the telegraph could work messages were daily sent in every direction, and after that mode of communication had ceased, messengers were constantly sent with letters.

Sir Henry was well aware of the critical position of Cawnpore, but, no doubt in unison with the general opinion here at that time, during May, 1857, did not at all anticipate so serious a catastrophe; one company of her Majesty's 32nd Regiment was, however, sent over to Cawnpore. Events have thus been briefly sketched to the end of May, 1857; the 30th of May opened a new scene in the drama.

On the 30th May the moveable column before alluded to, as sent towards Futtehghur through Oude, had reached Tiloe, a village four miles on the Lucknow side of Sundeela, and twenty-six miles from Lucknow; it must also be remembered that Captain Weston and Lieutenant Mecham were at Mulheeabad, fourteen miles from Lucknow. In both cases the troops were intimately associated with those in Lucknow, and the lives of the British officers then out with them in the district no doubt depended on the actions of the troops in Lucknow.

Providentially the 7th Oude Irregular Infantry, which had mutinied before, and a portion of which now formed the escort of Captain Weston and Lieutenant Mecham, together with some mounted police, remained faithful, and did not mutiny. The night I marched from Mulheeabad, Captain Weston and Lieutenant Mecham were in imminent peril, and once he summoned me back to his aid, but before we had retraced our steps two miles another messenger said the rebels had quieted; nothing but the bold determined firmness of Captain Weston overawed the 3,000 fanatic wretches who surrounded him.

Equally providential was it that the column at Sundeela did not at once receive the true account of the matter, but moving away day by day farther from Lucknow, remained in considerable ignorance altogether.

At 9 P.M., on the 30th, the troops in cantonments mutinied. Sir Henry, attended by Mr. Couper, Civil Service, the secretary, but in those times acting aide-de-camp in addition, at once went to the scene of action and ordered out the artillery and Europeans. The 71st, it is supposed, began it, joined by the 48th and some of the 7th Cavalry, the 13th Native Infantry remaining somewhat faithful, only a portion of it mutinying. As usual, bungalows were set fire to, and the usual confusion and rioting occurred. The Artillery and Europeans drove the mutineers back on their own lines, where they lurked about till morning. The 7th Cavalry came up from their lines at Moodkipoor, and patrolled between the iron and stone bridges to keep the city quiet, and prevent any attempt at communicating with the mutineers.

The troopers who were left in the cavalry lines on guard during the night, looted and burned the property they were acting guard over, and actually killed a fine young lad, called Raleigh, who had only joined the regiment a few days previously; he was quite a boy, and the ruthless spirit which prompted his murder showed the animus of the wretches: the lad had been unavoidably left in the lines during the night, and on attempting to join his corps in the morning, a trumpeter and a trooper killed him with their pistols and sabres.

Brigadier Handscombe, who was commanding the troops in cantonment, and had gone out to endeavour to quell them, was shot almost immediately; also Lieutenant Grant, of the 71st.

Early in the morning of the 31st the portion of the 7th Cavalry which had not then mutinied, and which had been on duty that night in the city, was sent towards its own cantonment, in which direction the mutineers had retired. As they entered on the plain, near their lines, some 1,500 mutineers and scoundrels attacked them in skirmishing order, compelling them to wait and send for the guns. About one-half of the cavalry deserted and joined the mutineers. The guns eventually came up, and a pursuit ensued, but the cavalry behaved badly, and nothing like a severe blow was struck on the mutineers, who made off towards Setapore. It appeared afterwards that about one-half of the 48th Native Infantry, half of the 71st, with a few men of the 13th Native Infantry, and two troops of the 7th Light Cavalry, had mutinied and gone off. All ladies and children were safely ensconced in the Residency, and the cantonments were held by some of the remaining troops, with a portion of the 32nd and the artillery.

Mr. Christian, writing from Setapore to me, thus describes succeeding events:—"Accounts are that the mutineers fled to Mahona, one march out of Lucknow in this direction, and then struck across the Goomtee, westward, for Mulheeabad. Immediately on the express reaching this, Lieutenant-Colonel Birch, with five companies of the 41st Native Infantry, marched for Peer Nuggur and will be at Bauree to-morrow. The colonel has written from Peer Nuggur, confirming the report that the mutineers have gone to Mulheeabad. All this district of

Setapore is quiet, and here we are fully prepared."

On the 1st of June news of the mutiny in Lucknow reached the moveable column near Sundeela. The men got the account nearly as soon as the letter from the secretary, Mr. G. Couper, C.S., reached me. That letter, written hurriedly on the moment, said, the 7th Cavalry generally had stood firm, as also the 48th, and their incessant and numerous inquiries of the men and officers were satisfactorily answered for the time; but numbers of runaway syces and attaches of the mutinous portion of the 7th Light Cavalry soon reached the column, and the men fully believed that there was doubt as to what their comrades in Lucknow had done. Their conduct changed from that date, and this event, no doubt, determined them to mutiny when they could get a convenient opportunity; but there was no hurry, the column was going to Futtehghur, all on the way to Delhi. The day previous to this news reaching the column, I had found it necessary to take the treasure from the Sundeela treasury. Villagers and rascals of all sorts were threatening it, and moreover it was a temptation to the men to take it by force if not allowed to have it quietly. It only amounted to 6,500 rupees, out of which, as the men were one month's pay in arrears, so much was paid them at once, leaving 1,200 rupees as a balance. This settled the difficulty, and as I did it as of my own accord on account of the risk of rebellious villagers seizing it, the men had no opportunity for outbreak, and were rather pleased at our apparent exceeding blindness, in taking the trouble to give them any pay at all, when they soon intended to mutiny. Doubtless they felt equally sure of the remaining 1,200 rupees, and any other odd sums in my treasure chest.

On the 2nd June, Mr. Capper, the deputy commissioner of Mulaon, writing to me, reported the Lucknow rebels to have reached Madhogunj, four coss from him, and begged me to aid him with the column; he also reported Mr. Christian having mentioned that Shahjehanpore had risen and had recommended him to entrench himself.

I at the same time received letters from the Futtehghur magistrate, begging me not to come near them; that he had heard of Captain Hayes's column and of ours, and felt certain that so long as no other troops came to Futtehghur, the 10th Regiment Native Infantry, would remain faithful, but that otherwise all would be hopeless.

Our column was now very awkwardly situated: mutineers and fugitives from Lucknow in its rear and flank, the Mulaon treasury standing temptingly ahead, and the Futtehghur magistrate saying, "Don't come near me;" the question to be solved was, where to put the column so that it could do no harm and not be led to mutiny at once.

It was found impossible to avoid passing Mulaon, but it was generally agreed to bivouac somewhere on the Ganges, out of the route of mutineers going north to Delhi, and where communications would be unlikely to occur with any other body of mutineers. By this time the officers with the column were all well aware of the unsatisfactory state of their men. But the elder officers, Captain Staples, of the cavalry, and Captain Burmester, of the 48th, refused to credit my warning that the men only bided their time. It was most natural that men with whom they had spent the best twenty years of their lives should be trusted; how could they not believe the daily oft-repeated assurance of fidelity? Were they not, as the snake-tongued villains said, "the children of their officers from whose hands they had fed for twenty years?" Thus by flattery and protestations they completely lulled to sleep every fear or suspicion. With the younger officers it was different; they had not the same associations to overcome, but they deliberately determined to die with their superiors. Lieutenant Boulton told me himself, when I warned him to be on his guard, "that he saw it clearly, but he had no wife, no family, he would never leave Dick Staples, and Dick did not believe his men would ever harm him." This he said with considerable emotion, and after some hours' consideration—it was a noble resolve. His letters to his brother officers, as stated to me by Mr. Martin, the deputy commissioner, fully showed the state of the men in his estimation, but so long as men daily protest faithfulness, it is not easy to credit treachery. The column was with difficulty safely pushed past Mulaon, where a company of the 41st Native Infantry guarded a small treasury. It was ascertained that had all agreed then, they would there have mutinied and taken the treasure, but the 41st preferred getting it all themselves, and so, after great dawdling and falling out of the ranks on false pretences, the column fairly marched from Mulaon towards the Ganges. At this time Mr. Capper, the deputy commissioner, thought his irregular levies staunch, and Lieutenant Inglis, commanding the 41st, had no open reason to doubt his company.

It was arranged with the officers of the column and myself, that the force, after passing Mulaon, should encamp on the banks of the Ganges, and that I should arrange with Mr. Capper to bring the necessary supplies there; this obliged Lieutenant Tulloch and myself to remain behind the column some hours. After great trouble and going into villages, purchasing supplies and loading on elephants what could be carried, we reached the banks of the Ganges at twelve the next day, only to find the column all across, except our own personal baggage, which appeared put down on an island in the middle of the Ganges. The Sikhs soon ascertained, and reported the cause of all this. The column had simply refused to halt on this side of the Ganges, and had easily persuaded their officers it would not signify crossing.

The troopers had by threats induced the small Sikh guard of some six or eight men with our baggage to go as far as the island in the middle of the river, and promise to bring it on when we arrived.

The twenty Sikhs with Lieutenant Tulloch and myself now spoke more openly. Some of our baggage guard had come back to us, and they said it was madness to go on. The men only wanted us across to complete the net, and then march to Delhi. I determined therefore not to cross, but to endeavour to get the officers to leave their men and come over to me; it is difficult to explain these things, but it was as plain as daylight that the men were not under control. I wrote to Major Marriott and the other officers, reminded them of the disposition shown by the men ever since leaving Sundeela, when they heard of the mutiny of their own corps, and implored them to leave the men, if they would not obey orders and march at once to Cawnpore, which was then quiet, as the troops must not go to Futtehghur.

Major Marriott sent for his native officers, who at once told him it was useless issuing such orders, for the men would not obey. The major used all proper efforts, but having utterly failed, and convinced himself the men were no longer under the control either of the native officers or of the European, he, after some hours' consideration, determined to recross the river and join me; at that time such was the state of the men that he was obliged to come over, leaving everything behind, except the clothes on his back. He brought with him Dr. Darby, the medical officer of the detachment.

The local position of the force across the river was most objectionable; all the country across the Ganges was alive with rumours and excitement, and the troops necessarily were in the way for temptation to reach them easily. I stayed, as I had arranged, till twelve o'clock at night, and then commenced our return march, purposing to pick up the officers at Mulaon, G. Capper, Esq., the civil officer, and Lieutenant Inglis, commanding a company of the 41st. There was no doubt this company would rise directly it suited them, and it was an object to be within reach. Except the twenty Sikhs, our Nujjeebs, numbering forty, were not to be depended on; the country was rising rapidly in our rear, not in absolute violence, but quietly arming; and villages, where all was quiet and agricultural, now mustered their armed men, and collected supplies for the coming storm, whatever it might be. Everywhere the roads were covered with stragglers rousing the country, and armed with many a plundered weapon of some sort or other.

The column across the river, it was ascertained, moved some four miles to Chobeypore, a village nearer the Trunk Road, and where the men could get better information of what was going on around them.

The date is not known, but probably on the 7th or 8th, it was elicited from the officers' servants who had escaped, that about three P.M., just after the officers had dined, the assembly sounded in both the cavalry and infantry lines. The officers sent to ask about it, but the native officers would not come. Lieutenant Martin, of the cavalry, got up to mount his horse,—for they had all ordered their horses to be saddled. As Lieutenant Martin walked towards his horse, a trooper approached, and led it away. Lieutenant Martin called to him; the trooper turned and fired at him: it is not known whether he was killed at once; reports said that others fired at the same time and killed him.

Lieutenant Boulton tried to assist Captain Staples away, who had received a wound, and could not ride his own horse. Lieutenant Boulton did get him up behind him, but Captain Staples was very heavy and fell. Nought remained for Lieutenant Boulton but to ride off. He did so, it is reported, and got away across country to Cawnpore: this, however, was not clearly corroborated. Of the infantry officers, no detailed account could be got, except that they there perished.

Having perpetrated this foul deed, the men marched to Delhi. Some three days after leaving the Ganges, a letter came from Sir Henry Lawrence, calling upon the officers to leave their men if they showed any signs of mutiny: it was too late, but anyhow their determination was to wait for open violence.

Our party marched towards Lucknow, having received orders to remain on the Lucknow side of Mulaon, sufficiently near for Mr. Capper to join, if necessary; this was afterwards unnecessary, as Mr. Capper joined us on the march.

Lieutenant Inglis remained a day or so with his company after Mr. Capper left, no doubt believing fully his men would never mutiny; they, however, one morning possessed themselves of the treasury, and Lieutenant Inglis joined my camp in a woman's doolie, or chair, carried by two men, having escaped from Mulaon, gone to sleep under a tree, being thoroughly plundered and threatened with death by a rajah, and eventually fed and sent to our party.

This little force had several threatened attacks, but none came off. The difficulty of getting supplies was considerable, but otherwise no particular impediments to our return march occurred. Very much was I indebted on several occasions to the zeal and energy of my assistant, Lieutenant Tulloch, whose ever ready cheerful aid was most valuable. At the town of Mohan, we seized two guns, spiked and threw them down a deep well. As we neared Lucknow Sir Henry Lawrence sent for me to arrange for our party with a slight increase, and with Captain Forbes, to remain out moving about near the Cawnpore road. We accordingly started, but were summoned in again almost immediately, as Sir Henry had abandoned the idea of keeping out any more native troops with European officers.

The Sikhs behaved admirably on this occasion; they had escorted safely five officers through a country up in arms, where we were obliged to march all night, and bivouac in the day near some small village, and they had been sorely tempted. All were rewarded on reaching Lucknow; yet, incredible as it may appear, their leader, a very fine young man, and some five or six others, all deserted during the siege of the "Baillie Guard."

I must now record events in Lucknow which occurred during the first three days of June. Numerous punishments of bad characters and executions of rebels and deserters took place, and it was intended to send a company of Her Majesty's 32nd on elephants to Setapore, which Sir Henry perceived would soon follow; but an attempt at an *émeute* on the part of the city people entirely prevented it. A number of bad characters, with green banners, collected in a part of the city called Moofteegunge, and in the neighbouring quarters they murdered a Mr.

Mendes, a clerk in one of the public offices, who, strongly against the advice of his friends, ventured into that part of the city with only three or four armed servants, and then they proceeded to attack the kotwallee, or chief police office of the city. The police, wonderful to relate, at once sallied out, met the rebels in Hussungunge, a public and rather open thoroughfare, attacked and dispersed them. On the police side four or five were killed and wounded, whilst the insurgents lost fifteen or twenty men. Numerous arrests followed this affair, and several executions were effected at the usual place near the fort of the Muchee Bhawun. At this time, during the first three days of June, evidence was so far obtained of an extensive conspiracy in the city and in the cantonments, as to convince the authorities that the volcano existed and was ready at any time to burst out, but not sufficiently conclusive to lead to the arrest of more than three principal men on whom suspicion rested. One was a man called Shurruffo Dowlah, and the other two were Rookoon-ood Dowlah and Mussee-ood Dowlah. Shurruffo Dowlah's arrest was but partial, and never completely carried out; various circumstances rendered it at that time inexpedient, and the evidence was not sufficiently convicting; but the two latter were arrested, and of these Rookoon-ood Dowlah died in captivity in the Residency, and Mussee-ood Dowlah was released on the security of Moomtaz-ood Dowlah. This incident, unsatisfactory in itself, is noted here to show how high as well as low in the city were banded with the army against us; and though the authorities had no doubt that a most extensive conspiracy existed, the traces of which they had partially detected in these high personages, yet never was any further information obtained whatever. A resident of the town, who had formerly been a tuhseeldar, gave this information through the kotwal, or head native police officer of the city, and there is no doubt of its truth.

It may be interesting to notice that the before-mentioned Shurruffo Dowlah was formerly, in the king's time, a very important man at court, and held the title of naib, or deputy; he was prime minister during the reign of Mahomed Alee Shah, and of his successor Umjud Alee Shah. During the whole period of the siege of Lucknow he took an active part in the rebel government against us, and finally perished in a mosque in the outskirts of the city, where he had lingered, in unison with the Fyzabad Moulvie and his adherents, after the British had taken the greater part of the city. The manner of his death was clearly ascertained by our troops, who, on approching the mosque, heard a scuffle within, and a great noise; the rebels fled hastily, leaving Shurruffo Dowlah murdered on the floor, with his head nearly severed from his body. He had several times, it appeared, been accused by them of selling them to the British, and, accordingly, they murdered him when the British came near him.

Referring back to the arrests before mentioned, some others were afterwards added to their number, and included Moostufa Alee Khan, the elder brother of the king, and the Rajah of Toolseepore (since dead), with two brothers connected with the royal family of Delhi. This, with the vigilance of the police, under Major Carnegie, kept the city tolerably quiet, but a new cause soon rose to add fuel to the already glowing fire of excitement.

The news from our out-station rapidly and efficiently brought in by the horse-dawk arrangements, made under the orders of Sir Henry by the deputy commissioner, Mr. Martin, showed that the mutiny at Lucknow had seriously affected them. Mr. Christian, the commissioner of Setapore, wrote cheerfully; but the rise and massacre of Shahjehanpore, combined with that of Lucknow, rendered the position of Setapore most critical. The following two letters written by him to me, then out in the district as political agent in charge of the column before mentioned, admirably describe the object of the moveable column, and also the position of Setapore, before the mutiny, with the preparation made to meet it:—

Setapore, May 28*th*,
Thursday, Noon.

MY DEAR HUTCHINSON,

I was delighted to hear that our scheme of a moveable column had been approved, and that you were actually engaged in organizing it; one elephant has already arrived, and I have written for four more, and hope to have in all three or four elephants here ready for you.

My object in writing now is to suggest that, as soon as your column is ready, you march *viâ* Mulheeabad and Sundeela, either to this or on at once to Sandee.

Mulheeabad has just been added to this division, and I do not know the place or people.

Besides Chowdree Mustafa Khan you mention, I hear that Yacoob Khan, formerly commandant of the Kazimee Pultun at Sundeela, is raising men near Mulheeabad, and there are lots of Puthâns in that town.

Sundeela is also a rather "Yagee" Mussulman town, and by coming *viâ* Mulheeabad to Sundeela, you will give confidence, and at Mulheeabad send for Chowdree Mustafa Khan and Yacoob Khan, having previously arranged to arrest them, if they refuse, and bring them along in all courtesy as prisoners.

Then you had better come to this from Sundeela, or go on to Sandee as you please.

I should certainly like you to come through those two towns, and "bone" those two men.

There is excitement in the Mulaon district, and if you would like to go off at once to Sandee from Sundeela, it would do good, and I would send the elephants to join you wherever you choose to name. I send this by sowars, as I am late for the post.

Yours sincerely,
(Signed) G. J. Christian.

Setapore, June 1st,
My dear Hutchinson, *Monday,* 9 p.m.

Your letter of the 31st ultimo has just reached me. Since you wrote, two events have happened, of one of which I sent you an account yesterday.

On Saturday night there was a mutiny at Lucknow, in which men from three regiments—the 71st (who began it), the 48th, and the 7th Light Cavalry—joined. They burnt down several bungalows, but failed to do more, as they were soundly thrashed out of cantonments, and hotly pursued by the Chief Commissioner with Hardinge's and some of Fisher's Horse. To finish this matter first, it would appear that a great slaughter was made of the mutineers who dispersed in their flight. The city remained perfectly quiet, and order was restored in cantonments when the chief wrote to me on Sunday morning.

The only casualties were Brigadier Handscombe, Lieutenant Grant, and Lieutenant Martin,* of the 7th Cavalry. My accounts are that the mutineers fled to Muhona, one march out of Lucknow in this direction, and then struck across the Goomtee westward for Mulheeabad.

Immediately on the express reaching this, Lieutenant-Colonel Birch, with five companies of the 41st Native Infantry, marched to Peernagur, and will be at Baree to-morrow.

The colonel has written from Peernagur, confirming the report that the mutineers have gone to Mulheeabad. All this district of Setapore is quiet, and here we are fully prepared.

I think the 41st Native Infantry will stand fast, unless they

* This was an error; Lieutenant Martin was then out with me; it was Cornet Raleigh, 7th Cavalry, who was killed.

are met and tampered with; they marched out in good spirits. If they do stand fast, all is well here.

If they go over, we know the worst. Even then I believe the 9th and 10th Oude Irregular Infantry and the military police will be firm.

The other event is, that on Sunday, at Shahjehanpore, the Europeans in church were attacked. Poor Ricketts, the magistrate, was killed, and Doctor Bowling and Ensign Spens badly wounded.

One report, or rather one letter, names Mrs. Ricketts as killed, but this, I think, is a mistake. Is she not in the hills?

The officers of the 28th Native Infantry, to the number of [nine], and five or eight ladies, escaped to the Rajah of Powaen; what part the regiment took is not mentioned, but they *must* have mutinied actively or passively.

I write *openly to you* in expressing *entre nous* my belief that Bareilly and Futtehghur are likely to follow.

At Mohumdee, Thomason and Orr are in the fort with two companies, 200 strong, of the 9th Oude Irregular Infantry, and half a company military police, and they have 200 men besides.

Thomason, on Sunday, wrote in a confident tone that all was quiet, and he could hold the fort, and believed in his men.

Here you know our position. I have placed all the ladies, children, and women, except some four who will not leave the lines of the 41st Native Infantry, in my house, and made all secure. I have brought up Hearsey, and the head-quarters have now—

9th Oude Irregular Infantry	250 recruits.
10th ,, ,,	330 ,,
Military Police	280
,, (new levies)	80
Chuprassies, &c.	200

We have four guns, and are placed, as you know, as represented in the accompanying sketch (*see* next page).

I now only wait for the attitude of the 41st Native Infantry.

If they are staunch and act against the insurgents, all is over, and we have no trouble; if they mutiny, I think the bulk of our force is staunch, and that the 41st Native Infantry will make a run of it, and not attack us.

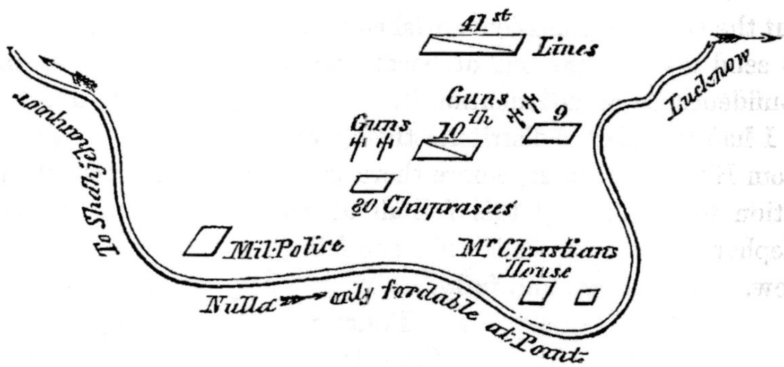

I am prepared to reinforce Mulaon or Mohumdee, but until there is a necessity, I wish to keep the force together. Its strength and mixture is our security. Now, as for you, I much fear that the news from east and west will affect your force, but it is right to state that Vanrennan, in writing from Lucknow, states that the 48th Native Infantry did not join, but were loyal to a man. Couper, at an *earlier* hour, writes that the greater part of the 48th did join; some of the 7th Cavalry joined, and some were very staunch. Now you can judge how news from east and west will affect your force.

I recommend that you do not halt at Mulaon. There the company 41st Native Infantry will be staunch till the head-quarters go (if they ever do), and with the two companies—4th Oude Irregular Infantry and forty of Fisher's Horse and Levies—there is a strong good force.

But your force at Mulaon may sorely try them.

I recommend you to march to Bawun *viâ* Soorsâ, and thence to Sandee. Avoid Bilgram, a Yagee Mussulman town, on the direct road from Mulheeabad to Sandee.

From Sandee, move in the direction of Nahtora, Konda, and Tandeeawun, but avoid Shahabad and Pyhanee—both bad Mussulman towns—and, on no account, go into Furruckabad. If the 10th Native Infantry have *not* mutinied, they are said to be ready to do so on the arrival of fresh troops.

I never asked for, nor do I want, a troop of the 7th Cavalry; but the Chief Commissioner wished me, on its arrival from you, to send it anywhere out of harm's way. This was written in confidence, so do not mention it.

I had intended to distribute them along my northern frontier from Bhira to Kheree, where there is no danger and no population to coerce, and this I shall do when they come. The elephants are being collected; one fell ill, and I have only one now. Write often and fully.

Yours sincerely,
(Signed) G. J. CHRISTIAN.

The foregoing sketch will give a general idea of the position Mr. Christian took up. He depended, as it has been seen, entirely on his local regiments, and, accordingly, posted them round him; his rear was safe from attack, protected by a deep nullah, fordable only at two or three points. It may be seen at a glance how such a position became a trap, directly his own men mutinied, but we must not therefore undervalue Mr. Christian's arrangements.

He was well aware that no aid could come to him from any quarter; he felt it his duty to stand firm at his post, and resist to the utmost the rapidly increasing mutiny. Lucknow had not fallen completely in its first throes; why should Setapore? It was possible that a remnant might remain faithful, and enable him either to hold his own or make a befitting retreat. His own district was in comparative quiet, and the loyalty protested by the local regiments was considerable. Determined as he was to stand and resist the mutiny, it was absolutely necessary he should trust some troops, and he therefore placed confidence in the local regiments, also raising a few levies of irregular armed men. All were stationed so as to command completely any advance of the 41st on the civil lines and the houses which contained the ladies (Mr. Christian's own house and his office); four guns were posted on that front, as shown in the plan, near the 9th and 10th Infantry. Some irregular levies were placed in Mr. Thornhill's and Captain Barlow's adjoining compound, and in Mr. Christian's own garden.

On the 27th May, about noon, the vacant lines of the 10th Regiment Military Police were fired by some miscreants; the men were put under arms, with some other irregulars, as a rise was anticipated, but all remained quiet, and the fire was speedily extinguished. The corps which enjoyed much confidence was the 10th Regiment. Three or four anonymous letters written in the Hindee character were brought by some men of this regiment to their officers. The letters stated that it was the intention of the 41st Native Infantry and the 9th Oude Irregular Infantry to make a simultaneous rise, and murder all the European and Christian community, but no hint was given as to time or date.

On the 2nd of June, the 10th Oude Irregular Infantry rejected some cartloads of flour, which had been sent for the use of the regiment by the kotwal of the city; the men said the flour was adulterated, and would destroy their caste if they used it; they also insisted on the whole of the flour being thrown into the river, which was done.

It is well to notice here how by little and little the sepoys tested their power, and felt their way to open mutiny; the rejection of the flour was no doubt a preconcerted plan.

On this same day, some men of this regiment plundered the fruit in the garden of the commissioner, Mr. Christian, and of some others. Lieutenant Greene, of the 9th Oude Irregular Infantry, and Mr. Bickers, late superintendent of Mr. Christian's office, went out and endeavoured to stop the sepoys, asking at the same time the cause of their irregularity. The answer was, they did but what many others were doing; and if wrong, they were very sorry.

Mr. Christian, it is said, paid little heed to this very remarkable and insubordinate proceeding, and some private accounts lament his doing so. A little reflection will show that it was but true wisdom. He had not the power to prevent it, he would not willingly hurry the bursting of the storm, and therefore to take no notice was simply the real wisdom of necessity. Preparations for flight evidently held no part, however justifiable they were or might be, in Mr. Christian's counsels, and in his high position, forgetting wife and children, he laboured as much to quell the but too natural fears of the European community, as to suppress by every means in his power that impending danger, the more dreaded because unseen, which gave rise to the fears of those around him. Possessed of far more abundant and more accurate information than others, he saw the whole danger, and felt *his* duty was to brave it. Pay was issued to all the troops present on this 2nd of June, and the detachments from the 2nd Military Police Regiment at Mohumdee, Mulaon, and the neighbouring districts, were ordered to rejoin their regiment,—their places being supplied at the various district police stations by irregular levies, raised for the occasion by the subordinate native civil officers.

It may be as well to mention here, that in order to give every feasibility and probability of success to the plan of fighting irregulars against regulars, Mr. Christian had sought to form his irregulars of many different classes, trusting they would not be so easily tempted to join the regulars in mutiny. For this reason he had raised some seventy or eighty Passees, and placed them along the banks of the "nullah" as guards; they had their favourite weapon, the bow and arrow.

By these arrangements the supposed enemy, the 41st, no doubt would have been well met at every point; but as all turned traitors, so the precautions of our countrymen did but render more sure their own destruction. At the eleventh hour only was it that the troops depended on moved against the unfortunate residents, with all the sleekness of Asiatic expression; their smooth-tongued protestations of loyalty found but too ready belief in the minds of their victims, and it is not the least remarkable feature of this and other mutinies of India that, as the cat dallies with the mouse, so did the mutineers dally until the last moment. Determined on mutiny from the beginning, they bided but their

6—2

own time, employing the interval, according to their character, in blinding, by all possible means, the eyes of those whose salt they had eaten.

It is well known to every resident of India, that the old servants of fifty years—twenty, perhaps, of which have been passed in your service—can, on the occasion of being robbed of a few rupees, or breaking a tea-cup, produce a flood of tears so copious that they bear comparison only to the excessive grief of human nature under some of its sorest trials; it may then be understood, be in some measure comprehended, that the old native officer who had seen sixty summers, as he stood with grey hair and streaming eyes in the presence of his old commander of thirty years' service, and there, in accents almost inarticulate with grief, besought, implored him not to mistrust, not to doubt the regiment they had both served in for so many years—I say it may be in some measure understood how that old man's pathetic appeal produced on the heart of his commanding officer an impression that the regiment after all was not so bad as was said, and that this old man, at any rate, was a firm old friend.

At 8 A.M. of the 30th June a Mahomedan subadar of the 10th Regiment Oude Irregular Infantry, called on Mr. Bickers, the superintendent of Mr. Christian's office, and after reprobating all the mutineers as cowardly wretches, professed himself a most faithful servant of the State, and declared that his regiment would be found faithful to the last. He then inquired Mr. Bickers' reasons for sending his family to the commissioner's house, and, stating that the act implied a suspicion of the loyalty of the 10th, which was not fair, urged him to bring them back again, and that if danger occurred he, the subadar, would protect them. So earnest was the man that he very nearly lulled all Mr. Bickers' suspicions to rest, but an all-merciful Providence defeated this diabolical attempt, for such it can only be designated, as future events too clearly showed.

It is worthy of notice that a scene similar to this actually occurred at Bareilly, on the occasion of the officers sending away their wives to prevent their massacre, and that had they listened to their men all would have been lost. The supposition that native officers so acting really believed their regiment would remain true, and did not know of the intended mutiny, is one with which one cannot rest satisfied for an instant; facts too clearly showed the contrary. Colonel Birch, commanding the 41st at Setapore, up to the last minute of his life, trusted his men. If confidence was wanted, they had it in abundance. He had led his men out in person against the Lucknow mutineers, and in every way always shown *he* did not doubt them.

The attitude, then, of Setapore was one of expectation; the ladies were collected in two communities, one in the civil lines, and the other in the military; the gentlemen of the civil lines being located in Lieutenant Lester's house. On the 2nd of June Colonel Birch, commanding the 41st Regiment Native Infantry, returned from the position he had held for a short time at Baree, on the Lucknow road (to prevent the Lucknow mutineers coming to Setapore).

On the 3rd of June, at sunrise, Major Apthorp, of the 41st, informed Mr. Christian that the men of the 41st were disaffected. Mr. Christian immediately went to see Colonel Birch, who, as yet, did not believe the disaffection general. The guns were at once loaded and primed, the 9th and 10th ordered to be ready, the police and irregular levies distributed here and there, and all felt some kind of confidence, as the only apparent danger was from the 41st. About 8 A.M., Major Apthorp came to Mr. Christian and said that the men would not be guided by him or listen to his exhortations; they had determined to mutiny. One company soon afterwards marched from their lines, and, taking the Lucknow road, went towards the treasury, whilst the rest of the regiment formed up and advanced in a threatening attitude on the local regiments, the 9th and 10th. It must be noted here that the gunners were all natives.

About this time Colonel Birch, Lieutenants Greene and Smalley, with the sergeant-major, went to the treasury also. The building was about one mile from the 41st lines, and about half a mile from the commissioner's house. Mr. Christian had previously ordered the late Lieutenants Lester and Dorin, with Captain Hearsey, to take every precautionary measure. He desired Captain Hearsey to increase the strength of the guard at his house, where all the ladies and children were. Captain Hearsey accordingly sent a strong party of the military police, and some twenty of those hastily raised irregular mercenaries called "Nujjeebs," thus unwittingly rendering but too certain the destruction of those victims by the very men who had solemnly sworn to protect them.

About an hour after the first act of mutiny, the march of the companies of the 41st to seize the treasure, Captain Hearsey was passed by Mr. Christian and Mr. Thornhill, both on horseback, going towards the treasury; they had hardly passed him a minute when Captain Hearsey heard firing in that direction, and those gentlemen cantered back to where Captain Hearsey was standing, and informed him that Colonel Birch and Lieutenant Graves had been shot by their men, and that he might presently expect an attack from them. Nothing clear is known of the fate of Colonel Birch, except that his men shot him at the treasury, whilst he, with a noble confidence, utterly lost on such wretches, continuing to point out to them the madness of their folly, and exhorting them to listen to his words, died trusting them to the last.

Just before the colonel was shot, Mr. Bickers, the superintendent of the commissioner's office, who had galloped over to the 41st lines, found all quiet; the sepoys said the colonel had gone to the treasury with some men.

Mr. Bickers also visited the house of the quartermaster sergeant of the 9th Regiment Oude Irregular Infantry; all was quiet there, according to Sergeant Abbott's account, who entirely trusted his own men.

The systematic plan of this mutiny merits attention: there was no extenuating feature here. Cursed by an avaricious furor, as well as by a mutinous spirit, these petted soldiers quietly possessed themselves of the treasure first to prevent others doing so, and then deliberately commenced the work of murder.

Lieutenant Graves was not shot, as Mr. Christian had supposed, but only wounded; he was, providentially, able to gallop back to his lines and give warning to all his brother officers and their families, who at once started off for Lucknow.

Very soon after the shots were heard at the treasury, musketry was heard in the lines of the 9th Oude Irregular Infantry, and a sepoy running from the regiment to Captain Hearsey, informed him, in breathless haste, that the men had shot Captain Gowan and Dr. Hill. This appears to have been the signal for the concerted rise of all the irregulars. Quartermaster-Sergeant Abbott escaped from the 9th Oude Irregular Infantry to Lieutenant Lester's house, with a severe flesh wound in the arm; this was bound up for him by Mr. Bickers. Some of the Christian community, with Sergeant Abbott, now crossed the stream in rear of the position before the troops in the garden and on its banks had themselves joined in the mutiny, and thus escaped into the jungles.

Mr. Christian, on hearing the musketry on the 9th Oude lines, took his rifle and advanced towards the military police, commanded by Captain Hearsey. Mr. Christian and also Mr. Thornhill had, a short time previous, been begged by Captain Hearsey to hurry home and get the ladies and children across the stream in their rear, their only remaining chance of safety. They did go quickly home, but could scarcely have had time to make any arrangements, when Captain Hearsey saw the 10th Regiment Oude Irregular Infantry give a shout and charge right into Mr. Christian's garden: that instant all the irregular lines joined in the hellish massacre—all was lost, and flight only remained. To give a connected account of the events of the next twenty minutes in this part of the station cannot be expected, but the following is all that can be ascertained with apparent truthful evidence to support it.

Mr. Christian, finding all were turning against him, walked deliberately down towards the river, preceded by his wife, with an infant in her arms, their other child being already across the river with the nurse, or being taken across by Sergeant-Major Morton. It is not quite certain whether Mr. Christian had with Mrs. Christian reached the other side of the stream, or only reached the bank on this side; I think Lieutenant Lester, when in the Baillie Guard, told me he had seen Mr. Christian on the other side.

If so, as evidence shows they were together, they had just crossed and that would be all, when Mr. Christian fell dead, pierced by many balls. Nobly had he braved the storm, nobly he died. His poor wife, from the evidence elicited, appears to have been a little in advance of him, and as he fell on his face, shot from behind by the traitors around his own house, she had sat down beside him with the little babe in her arms. At this moment the infernal din is portrayed as baffling all description, and yet a more exquisitely touching scene can hardly be conceived than the one before us. Her own house behind her in flames, casting its lurid glare on the little stream between them, which, already copiously stained with the blood of her race, offered but a temporary obstacle to some 1,200 fiends, who, with an incessant yelling, shouting, firing, rained from their muskets death on all around her; still, there sat that Christian mother with her babe, a little moment, unheeded and unheeding, for before her lay him dead. It was *but* a moment; the savages knew no mercy; in the full swing of passions unrestrained, they found a lower depth amidst the lowest hell: all sexes were alike to them, and age brought no exemption—the infant and its mother were numbered with the dead.

Of Mr. and Mrs. Thornhill, the account is unsatisfactory; but all concur in showing that they met their death either in crossing or across the stream. Their little girl, Cathy Thornhill, is supposed to have been temporarily rescued by some one of the parties who did escape, but to have died under subsequent fatigue. Little Sophy Christian, who is mentioned to have previously crossed the river with her nurse, was eventually taken care of by Sergeant-Major Morton, as the nurse was shot by one of the million bullets flying about.

Sir Mountstewart Jackson and one sister, with Sergeant-Major Morton and little Sophy Christian—who died afterwards in captivity in the Kaiser Bagh, at Lucknow, escaped to the Mitholee Rajah, where they found Captain and Mrs. Orr, who had escaped the massacre of the Shahjehanpore fugitives. It is not on record how Sir M. Jackson and his party managed to reach Captain Orr, as the Shahjehanpore fugitives were massacred in Oude. It may be as well to note here that all that is known about them will be found in an account farther on in this work, written by Captain Alexander Orr.*

Lieutenant Lester told me that he succeeded in reaching the jungle in safety, and he there met

* A surviving brother of the captain here mentioned.

Quartermaster-Sergeant Abbott; with him he wandered for some hours, and, strange to say, either on that or the next day, a native told them of an European woman and child being in the jungles, hiding. The man, on being requested, took them to her, and Sergeant Abbott saw before him his wife and child. Mr. Bickers, the superintendent of Mr. Christian's office, got safely across the river, under a shower of bullets, with his wife and three children, one only eight days old.

Mrs. Morton, wife of Sergeant-Major Morton, and one child, also Mrs. Brown (wounded), sister-in-law of Sergeant Keough, 9th Oude Irregular Infantry, and one child, and Sergeant Anderson, 10th Oude Irregular Infantry, all crossed safely.

Mr. Bickers and family reached Lucknow on the 8th June, after experiencing great hardships, and Lieutenant Lester, with the others named above, reached two days later.

To Lieutenant Lester's admirable knowledge of the country and the people, may be attributed very greatly their safe arrival. He at once led the way to a neighbouring zemindar (name unknown), and obtained food and shelter for immediate wants, besides the ways and means for their being passed on from one man to another, until they reached Lucknow.

It may not be inadmissible to mention here, that Lieutenant Lester was killed very shortly after the siege of Lucknow began, about the 18th or 19th of July, 1857. I saw him directly after he was hit; the ball, one of the many flying about from all sides, struck him in the back near the neck, and injured the spine, so that the lower limbs became powerless. At the time he was on the top of a house called "Mr. Gubbins' stables," and doing his best to aid in keeping down the fire of the besiegers. The spine was injured, and he sank very gradually, getting weaker and weaker; it was on the second or third day after being wounded that, having been raised up to make his bed comfortable, very shortly after we had laid him down again he passed away almost imperceptibly. Mr. Christian told me, on a former occasion, that Lieutenant Lester was one of the best and most promising young officers he had met with.

Another party, consisting of Mrs. Dorin, widow of Lieutenant Dorin, 10th Oude Irregular Infantry; Mr. Dudman, his wife, mother, mother-in-law, and four children; Mr. Morgan and wife; Mrs. Horan and five children; Mrs. Keough, widow of Sergeant Keough, 9th Oude Irregular Infantry, and child; Mr. Birch, son of Colonel Birch, commanding at

Setapore; Miss Birch, daughter of ditto; and Mrs. Ward, all reached Lucknow on the 28th June, having been protected by a zemindar of Ramkote, who was liberally rewarded by Sir Henry Lawrence, K.C.B. Mrs. Cranenburgh, Mrs. Owen and her two sons, and Mr. Scott, preferred staying with the zemindar at Ramkote, so it is said. Another account states that Mr. and Mrs. Cranenburgh were shot as they endeavoured to escape from their own house. Mr. Phillips, a clerk, and his wife escaped by native disguises, and actually, after various escapes, succeeded in reaching our column, which went from Lucknow in April towards the position of the rebels on the Gogra, thus having been ten months in concealment. The list of killed at Setapore is as follows :—

Name	Corps	Number
Mr. and Mrs. Christian, 1 child, and a European nurse		4
Mr. and Mrs. Thornhill ,, ,, ,,		4
Lieutenant-Colonel Birch Lieutenant Smalley Sergeant-Major Middleton	41st N. I.	3
Lieut. Graves, wife, and child Dr. Hill Sergeant-Major Keough, and two children Lieutenant Greene	9th Oude Irr. Infantry	8
Lieutenant Dorin Lieut. Snell, wife and child	10th Oude Irr. Infantry	4
Mr. Cranenburgh, clerk		1
	Total persons	24

The officers of the 41st at the other end of the station, we have noticed, escaped safely into Lucknow, some few of the sepoys escorting them a little way. We must now return to Captain Hearsey, who was left with his military police.

Captain Hearsey thus describes his position and subsequent wanderings :—

The cruel work of carnage in the civil part of the station had been commenced by the 10th Oude Irregular Infantry, but all others, as they arrived in succession, joined in the ruthless slaughter without exception or distinction. The din created by continued discharge of musketry for some time, the shouting of men and general conflagration of the houses and buildings, baffles all description; in fact, the whole place appeared like one pandemonium.

About 2 P.M., we were removed from under the tree to the late Captain Barlow's house, which had not been burnt till that time. Whilst there, my kitmutgar came in and informed me that he had seen poor Miss Jackson and another lady concealed in a bush on the other side of the river. I instantly started up, but Subadar Rugnath Sing and the men would not allow me to leave the house. However, I earnestly begged—since their intentions appeared friendly, and to save my life—either to enable me to effect the rescue of these ladies or perish in the attempt, on which some men ran out in the direction pointed, and in a very short time brought Miss Jackson and Mrs. Greene—the latter, wife of Lieutenant Greene, second in command of the 9th Oude Irregular Infantry.

Towards evening, I obtained a covered cart, called a bhylee, belonging to one of my servants. In this I put the two ladies,

Sergeant-Major Rogers, his son and wife, and assuming a native disguise, accompanied by some of the men, I marched towards the camp of the mutinous troops, which was pitched on the parade ground and topes adjoining. Owing to the confusion which prevailed, I succeeded in reaching the neighbourhood without detection, and put up under a tree near the military police. This measure I was obliged to adopt by the advice of Subadars Rugnath Sing and Madho Misser, who represented that any attempt on my part to escape at that critical moment would be fraught with imminent danger, as numberless parties of marauders from the regiments were out in pursuit of fugitives and plunder, to wait till it was dark, and that they would arrange about my departure.

The native officers of the 41st Native Infantry and the other regiments, notwithstanding the precaution above related, having by some means received information that my life had been spared, sent a deputation, saying, "that as *they* had murdered all their officers, it was imperatively necessary that the military police must either follow their example, or deliver me up a prisoner to them." On this being refused, the mutineers, apprehensive of causing dissension at so early a period, directed that the point in dispute should be settled by punchait, or arbitration, of a certain number of native officers from each regiment, at 9 P.M.

Subadars Rugnath and Madho Misser came and informed me of the circumstance, recommending an immediate departure, it being very near the time, and the night perfectly dark. Before the assembling of the council, I was enabled to leave. Placing the two ladies, Mrs. Rogers, and her son, on my elephant, the sergeant-major and myself mounted on horseback, we left for the north about 9 P.M. Madho Misser Subadar and fifteen men accompanied as an escort. My arms, which had been taken away at the commencement of the massacre by Subadar

Rugnath and six men, were restored; but the rest of my property, to a very considerable amount, fell into the hands of the mutineers.

We travelled all night, and by sunrise arrived at the village of Oael. I was refused admittance into the fort by Rajah Unrood Sing's people; but as the ladies were suffering much from fatigue and want of sleep, I sent a man, begging permission to be allowed to rest ourselves for a couple of hours. Even this request, though trifling enough, was refused. With much difficulty I obtained two of his followers, in order to secure us a safe passage through his district. Accompanied by these (the subadar and men having left us here), we pushed on towards the north, and reached a small fort near the Chowka River late in the evening. After a night's rest, we crossed over and marched to Baragaon. During the night, the elephant broke loose and disappeared; in consequence of which accident, I was obliged to halt for two or three days. Whilst at this place, I received a letter from the late Mr. H. Gonne, who had been informed of my flight, mentioning that himself and Captain Hastings had been joined by Messrs. Brand and Carew from Shahjehanpore, and that they were going down to Calcutta. He wished me to meet him at Mullapore without delay, as he had boats in readiness for the trip.

A day previous to this, I had written to Raj Aunut Sing, uncle to the Dhouraira Rajah, who sent down his elephant, a native palkee, and two tats; these were found awaiting our arrival across the Oorra River; and we continued our march to Mutteeara village, the place of residence belonging to the Rajah. We remained here about ten hours, and in the evening, accompanied by Raj Aunut Sing, went down by the river Kowreeally, and reached Mullapore next day, where we met the late Mr. H. Gonne.

The party now consisted of eleven persons, as marginally noted,* including myself.

Boats having been kept in readiness, we got on board during the night, on our way for Calcutta. Arriving at Rampore on the second day, we were kindly received by Thakoor Gooman Sing, who, after giving rest and refreshments in his place, informed us that a passage down by the river would be very unsafe, owing to the ghauts being narrowly watched by the mutineers. Mr. Cunliffe and others, who were going on to Lucknow from Baraitch, had been murdered whilst crossing at Byram Ghaut only the day previous. This disheartening news made us retrace our steps by land towards Mutteeara. On arrival, Fukeroodeen Khan, the government agent, received us in the name of the Ranee and the young Rajah, gave every assurance of safety and protection, telling the late Mr. Gonne that, on the approach of any danger, we should have timely notice, and boats would be kept in readiness to send the party across into the jungles, where we should be perfectly safe from pursuit.

We remained at this place for nearly two months. At the end of the period, in the early part of August, about 300 men of Girdharra Sing's regiment arrived from Lucknow, sent by the rebels then surrounding the garrison in Baillie Guard, to take us in. For two days we remained armed, and kept watch the whole night, refusing to go; but finding that Fukeroodeen Khan and the Ranee would neither assist nor allow us to escape, we began to suspect treachery. At last—seeing no other alternative, and as a last resource—a sort of compromise

* Miss Jackson, Mrs. Greene, Mrs. Rogers, Mr. H. Gonne, Capt. Hastings, Mr. Brand of Shahjehanpore, Mr. Carew of the same place; Sergeant-Major Rogers, 2nd Military Police; Mr. Brown, writer in Mr. Gonne's office; and J. Sullivan, step-son of Sergeant Rogers.

was made with the leader of these mutineers, Bunda Hussun, of Tumbour; and the party, after nearly a week's delay, marched towards Lucknow. Fukeroodeen Khan, with 400 men of the Ranee's, was also sent. On our second march from Mutteeara, Takoor Dabee Sing, a respectable zemindar in the Dhouraira Rajah's service, came in the evening, and confirmed our former suspicions, saying, "the Ranee and the government agent had formed a collusion with Bunda Hussun, and deliberately sold us to the rebels; that the agreement signed by the latter, allowing us to retain our arms, would be violated on arrival at Esanuggur."

This alarming piece of intelligence put the party on their guard. We held a consultation, and flight was decided upon. Next evening, finding an opportunity, a few valuables were secured; amongst the number, I carried my diary and some other papers. We placed the two ladies and the sergeant-major's wife on the late Mr. Gonne's elephant, and, mounting our horses, fled towards Khyreegurh, *en route* to Rajah Koolraj Sing's place, Kullooapore. Travelling all night and till 2 P.M., the party reached Bunbeerpore, a village in Rajah Rundhooj Sahaee's district. Here we dismounted to have refreshments, and give our jaded animals some rest. Whilst at meals, several villagers came in, running to give notice that about 300 men of Dhouraira, sent in our pursuit by the Ranee, were within a short distance. Instantly leaving the village and proceeding farther to the north, we arrived on the banks of the Mohan River about an hour before sunset, but could not get the ferry boat. The late Mr. Gonne proposed going up the stream, two miles to the west, where, he said, the Kowakhaira Ghaut might be found fordable. This also proved a failure, owing to the river having risen much. In the midst of a dense high grass and tree jungle, drenched to the skin from the pouring rain, since leaving Bunbeerpore, the position of the party, especially of the poor ladies, was uncomfortable to an extreme.

Whilst deliberating how to get across, suddenly a shout was raised; our pursuers, under cover of the brushwood, had gained upon us. Fastening the horses in a neighbouring hollow, we took up position behind trees. Presently the enemy opened a fire of matchlocks and commenced advancing, but very cautiously, as they knew we were all armed with good double-barrelled rifles. When within fifty yards, I obtained a glimpse of the leader and fired: the shot took effect, which checked their further proceeding. Meanwhile, the ladies, who had continued mounted on the elephant, and Mr. Carew with them, went off towards the west when the firing commenced; the rest of the party also retired, the late Captain Hastings and myself remained back to bring up the rear. We followed the tracks of the elephant for a considerable distance, but from the nature of the ground and the approaching darkness, the traces became more and more indistinct every moment. The late Captain Hastings suggested: "It is more than probable that Mr. Carew has taken the ladies to Rajah Rundhooj Sahaee's place;" for he always used to speak of him as a very great friend, therefore it was useless our following, as, owing to the cause above mentioned, we should never be able to overtake them, but very likely fall a prey to tigers or wild elephants. This made us decide upon taking shelter in a patch of grass on the banks of the river.

The horses and property left in the hollow were of course plundered when the enemy came up to the spot, as, for safety's sake, we were obliged to abandon all.

The late Captain Hastings and myself, not being able to overtake either the elephant or the other members of the party, swam across the river at 8 P.M., and remained under a tree during the night. Next morning we pushed on towards the direction of Kullooapore. Barefooted, and with scarcely any clothing, we reached the village of Sonapatha. This place belongs to Rajah Koolraj Sing, of Pudnaha. His karinda, or head man, supplied us with food, and gave the loan of two tats, which enabled us to prosecute our journey. Here we met Mr. Brand and Sergeant-Major Rogers. These also had swum the river in company with Mr. Brown, the writer; but, unfortunately, before the latter could gain the shore, an alligator pulled him in. Exhausted and foot-sore, we reached Kullooapore late in the evening, where the late Mr. Gonne joined us on the day following.

Having learnt from Sergeant-Major Rogers that the two ladies, Mr. Carew, Mrs. Rogers, and her son, were still in the forest, we got Rajah Koolraj Sing's uncle to send out parties in that direction. In the evening they came back, after a fruitless search. Although disappointed in the first instance, we halted for two days, sending out men well acquainted with every part of the jungle; but these also, I regret to observe, returned without gaining any satisfactory information.

The Dhouraira Ranee's followers, meanwhile, having learnt of our being at Kullooapore, came across the river, and were within a mile of the place, when intelligence was brought us during the night. We fled towards the forest of Seeshapanee, and remained concealed there for a couple of days. On the third, a jemadar of Rajah Koolraj Sing took us to Bulchoura, and from thence to Dholee Kote in the Nepaul hills. From the effects of the deadly climate and recent sufferings, the whole of the party, now reduced to five persons, was laid up with jungle fever. The Rajah showed every kindness and attention; he furnished us with clothes, food, and shelter —the latter, though merely a grass hut, was prized as the greatest comfort; for during the past week, our only canopy had been the heavens, and this during the most inclement part of the season.

Some days after our arrival at Dholee Kote, we heard a report about the ladies and the others who had got separated on the banks of the Mohan from the party, of their having fallen into the hands of the Dhouraira people, and taken back to Mutteeara, from whence they had been forwarded to Lucknow. Further particulars regarding the facts, or of their fate, we did not hear, nor had we the means to ascertain. The late Mr. Gonne, after twelve days' sickness, died of the jungle fever at this place. For upwards of three months, our party, now diminished to four, continued to reside in these hills; after which we came down to Bulchoura with the Rajah and his family, and lived in the Turaee. To avoid observation or inquisitive inquiries of the people belonging to the plains, our reed hut was constructed in a very remote part of the forest, far from any habitation. It is needless to add that our sufferings, both mental and physical, notwithstanding the Rajah's kind attention during our stay in this unhealthy place, were very great. Here the late Captain Hastings died on the 28th of December, 1857. About the latter end of this month, the Rajah received an order, signed by Shurfood Dowlah, saying, that the Durbar had received authentic information from the Ranee of Toolseepore, that he *still* gave protection to five Europeans in his district, and "that he must either send them in, or their heads, without delay."

Moreover, a letter which I had received from Mr. Wingfield, commissioner of Goruckpore, sent through the Rajah of Bulrampore, made us decide upon leaving our retreat for that place, the road being now practicable through the Nepaul hills. Mr. Brand and Sergeant-Major Rogers, being still weak from continued illness, were sent by the Rajah to the nearest military post in Nepaul, called Dyluck, and from thence to be forwarded by the authorities to Bootwell.

Being myself anxious to reach in time to accompany Jung Bahadoor's force into Lucknow, I made a short cut, travelling along by the bed of the Bubye, I managed to reach Sirreegounth, which is three marches from Lulleeana. On arrival, a party of hill-men, just arrived, informed me that the pass of Bootwell was blockaded by 20,000 rebels, led by Gooroopershad of Nepaul, and several relations of Jung Bahadoor, who were in command at Palpa and Pewthana, had been put in confinement by the Gorkha regiments. This startling news was confirmed by the karinda of the Ranee of Sirreegounth, which induced me to return to Bulchoura.

Oude and Rohilcund being still in possession of the rebels, I was unable to make my way direct to Lucknow; therefore, assuming the disguise of a native trooper in want of service, I marched towards Burrumdeo; passing through a great portion of the Oude Turaee, and undergoing many hardships, I ultimately reached the place in twelve days, where I met General Krishndooj of Nepaul. He received me most kindly and enabled me to proceed. On the 29th of January, 1858, I arrived at Loohoo Ghaut, and from thence, after a tedious journey across the hills, *via* Nynee Tal, Mussoorie, and Meerut, I reached Lucknow.

The next on the list of mutinies in Oude is Fyzabad.

The following account by Captain Reid, deputy commissioner of Fyzabad, gives considerable information regarding this mutiny:—

By the beginning of June, in the absence of any decisive

news from Delhi, it became evident that Fyzabad, with all the out-stations (in none of which were any European troops) must fall; though, as usual, the troops, consisting of a horse battery, 22nd Native Infantry, 6th Local Infantry, and a squadron 15th Irregular Cavalry, were most vehement in their protestations of loyalty to the last.

We at first intended to endeavour to hold the city against the mutineers, with the aid of the friendly zemindars and native pensioners; and, with this view, Captain Thurburn, special assistant commissioner, laid in supplies, and partly fortified the walled enclosure in which his residence was situated; but we were compelled to abandon this intention, as we found that the zemindars, however well disposed, would not fight against disciplined troops with guns.

On the 5th of June, I think, the late lamented Colonel Goldney, commissioner of the division, told me he had received instructions to direct me to send all the ladies and children into Lucknow. I replied that it was too late, as they could not be sent with safety through the Durriabad district, which was in a very disturbed state; a tuhseeldar having already been murdered, and that, besides, I was in hourly expectation of hearing of the mutiny of the Durriabad troops.

Prior to this, talookdars Rajah Maun Sing, Oodres Sing, Thakoornaryun Rughonauth Koonwur, Meer Baqur Hoosain, and Nadir Shah, had sent to offer an asylum to one or all of the civil officers' families; they all spoke of the mutiny as a certainty.

The Mahunts, too, of the famous Hunooman Ghurree, from the first exerted themselves to keep the troops steady, assuring them that the outbreak was but a puff of wind, which would soon pass away, and warning them that, if they proved false to their salt, they would have reason to bitterly regret their treachery. They now offered to receive any Europeans who might seek their protection, and, at the suggestion of Colonel Goldney, I sent them a thousand rupees to meet any necessary expenditure. These men, as well as the talookdars above mentioned, have all, I fear, since turned against us.

Of the above, Rajah Maun Sing was by far the most influential, and he alone had the power to afford protection to all the ladies and children of cantonments and the city; he was then in close but honourable confinement, having been placed under arrest by the commissioner, in obedience to orders from Lucknow. I was much opposed to this step, as, whatever may have been Maun Sing's conduct since, I had every reason to believe that he was then well affected to our Government.

Believing that Maun Sing was both able and willing to protect the ladies and children, and seeing no other means of insuring their safety, I proposed to send them to his fort of Shahgunj, twelve miles south of Fyzabad. The commissioner agreed to this proposal, and authorized me to release Maun Sing from arrest, and also to provide funds for the payment of men to garrison his fort.* I therefore proceeded, accompanied by Captain Orr, assistant commissioner, to the building—a house of his own—where Maun Sing was. He reiterated his offers of protection to the families of the civil officers, but made some demur about those of officers in cantonments, as receiving them would render futile any attempt at secrecy, and greatly increase the hazard of the undertaking.

* Note by Captain Hutchinson:—"I must remark here that Maun Sing was in confinement on a revenue question, when Capt. Alexander Orr, the assistant commissioner, who had known him for several years, begged his release, and it was entirely owing to Maun Sing's former long acquaintance with Captain Orr under the old *régime* that Maun Sing first offered to save Captain Orr's wife and children, and afterwards was induced to extend his protection to the large number he saved."

Of course, we told him we could not accept this limited offer; and, after some discussion, he agreed to receive all, on condition that the move from cantonments should be made quietly and secretly, not only because he doubted whether the troops would allow the officers' families to go, but because he required time to collect men and mature his own arrangements.

Captain Orr and I then repaired to cantonments where all the officers were assembled, and communicated Maun Sing's offer, with the condition attached to it. We suggested that the ladies should go out, as usual, in the evening, for a drive, and, instead of returning, proceed direct to Shahgunj.

The officers doubted the practicability of the scheme, and also urged that it would have a bad effect in exasperating the men, as we had no immediate apprehension of an outbreak. It was agreed to defer the departure of the ladies for a day, to give time to consider the matter, and to sound the troops.

Next morning, Mrs. Mills, wife of Major Mills, of the Artillery, determined to join our party, and came to Captain Thurburn's house in the city, but afterwards changed her mind and returned. All the other ladies, having some distrust of Maun Sing, decided on remaining in cantonments.

Arrangements were thus made to send our—*i. e.*, the civil officers'—families to Shahgunj on the night of the 7th; and in the evening I rode down to cantonments to communicate our plans to the officers, and to ask their final resolution. All declared they would retain their families in cantonments, except Captain Dawson, executive engineer, who, with his wife and four children, accompanied me home. They, with their families went off, as arranged, during the night, and reached Shahgunj in safety.

On the morning of the 8th, Corporal Hurst, of the Sappers, with his wife and child, and all the staff sergeants' wives and children, came to my house, and I sent them also off to Shahgunj, under escort of a party of trusty zemindars.

The crisis was now rapidly approaching; the district was full of mutineers from Azimghur, Benares, and Jaunpore; their emissaries reached the lines in the forenoon, and called on the troops to declare for them. I was told they had previously received a perwana from the King of Delhi, setting forth that he had possession of the whole country, and summoning them to join his standard. On that day, 8th June, I wrote my last report to Lucknow, stating that I had no hope that the outbreak could be staved off any longer.

During the day, I issued a month's pay to the zemindaree levies, about 400 strong, and about 100 native pensioners, and sent 14,000 rupees to Shahgunj; I also had the most valuable records secreted in the Waseeka buildings, a walled enclosure occupied by female relatives of the ex-king, subsisting on the interest of money invested in government papers, the safest and most convenient place I could think of at the time.

Colonel Goldney, commissioner and superintendent, remained in the city throughout the 8th, but in the evening returned to the lines of the 22nd Regiment Native Infantry, which he had formerly commanded, and I never saw him again.

The troops broke out in open mutiny on the night of the 8th June. They did not go through the form of pretending a grievance, but said they were strong enough to turn us out of the country, and intended to do it. The 15th Irregular Cavalry, particularly the rissaldar in command, left no means untried to induce the other regiments to murder their officers; but the Artillery, 22nd Native Infantry, and 6th Local Infantry, not only refused to injure the Europeans, but even gave them money, and assisted them in procuring boats to proceed down the Ghogra.

The following officers embarked in four boats, and dropped

down the river on the 9th, a little before sunrise. (*Vide* detailed account of Sergeant Busher.)

IN No. 1 BOAT.

Colonel Goldney, Commissioner of Fyzabad.
Lieutenant Currie, Artillery.
Lieutenant Cautley, 22nd Native Infantry.
Ensign Ritchie, 22nd Native Infantry.
Lieutenant Parsons, 6th Oude Local Infantry.
Sergeant-Major Matthews, 6th Oude Local Infantry.
Sergeant Edwards, Artillery.
Sergeant Busher, Artillery.

No. 2 BOAT.

Major Mills, Commanding Artillery.
Lieutenant and Adjutant Bright, 22nd Native Infantry.
Mrs. Hollum.
Quartermaster-Sergeant Russel, 22nd Native Infantry.
Bugler Williamson, Artillery.

No. 3 BOAT.

Colonel O'Brien, Commanding 6th Oude Local Infantry.
Lieutenant Gordon, 2nd in command, 6th Oude Local Inf.
Assistant-Surgeon Collison, 6th Oude Local Infantry.
Lieutenant Anderson, 22nd Native Infantry.
Lieutenant Percivall, Artillery.

No. 4 BOAT.

Lieutenant English, 22nd Native Infantry.
Lieutenant Lindesay, 22nd Native Infantry.
Lieutenant Thomas, 22nd Native Infantry.

The officers in No. 3 boat all reached Dinapore, though not without encountering great danger and difficulties. Of those who embarked on Nos. 1, 2, and 4, Sergeant Busher alone escaped. Colonel Goldney, Lieutenant Bright, Sergeant-Major Hollum, Quartermaster-Sergeant Russel, were all murdered by the 17th Native Infantry mutineers. Major Mills, Lieutenant Currie, and Lieutenant Parsons, were drowned. Lieutenants English, Lindesay, Cautley, and Thomas, and Ensign Ritchie and Sergeant Edwards, Artillery, were murdered by the villagers of Mahadubbur, in Goruckpore.

Colonel Lennox, with his wife and daughter, left Fyzabad, by boat, some hours after the others, and succeeded in reaching Goruckpore in safety: he has published an account of his adventures.

On a sixth boat embarked Captain Morgan, 22nd Native Infantry, and his wife and child; Lieutenants Fowle and Ouseley, and Assistant-Surgeon Daniel, of the 22nd Native Infantry. They suffered great hardships and privations; were plundered and maltreated on their voyage down the river. They all, however, eventually reached Gopalpore, and thence escaped to Chupra.

Mrs. Mills, with three children, attempted to conceal herself, I believe, in the city of Fyzabad, in the house of a havildar of the battery; but, as he refused to supply her with food, she was obliged to disclose herself to the leader of the mutineers, who gave her some money, and sent her across the Ghogra into the Goruckpore district. Here she is said to have wandered for eight or ten days from village to village. She appears to have received no assistance whatever from the police, who might easily have either sent her into Goruckpore, or have given information to the magistrate there. Mrs. Mills was a very delicate lady, and her sufferings must have been terrible. Her youngest child died from the exposure. At last Rajah Maun Sing, hearing there was an English lady in distress, sent for her, provided for her wants, and, after a few days' rest, sent her with the European sergeants' wives into Goruckpore.

The mutineers of Fyzabad first plundered about two lakhs and 20,000 rupees of treasure, and then followed the usual practice of releasing the prisoners in gaol. Among them was Sikunder Shah, a fanatic moulvie, who had endeavoured to excite rebellion in the city of Fyzabad in February, and who had been captured by a party of the 22nd Native Infantry, under Lieutenant Thomas. This officer and some sepoys were wounded on the occasion, and some of the moulvie's followers were killed, and himself and others wounded. This moulvie was chosen by the mutineers as their leader: he is even now a man of some note among the rebels.* The ringleaders of the mutiny were the rissaldar of the 5th Troop 15th Irregular Cavalry, and Duleep Sing, subadar of the 22nd Native Infantry, a Chowhan Rajpoot, of Burragaon, in the Fyzabad district. I have heard from different quarters that the rissaldar was killed at Lucknow while leading one of the attacks on the Residency.

All the civil officers dined at Captain Thurburn's on the evening of the 8th. After dinner, Mr. Bradford returned to the kutcherry in the belief—which the result proved well founded—that the men of the 22nd Native Infantry, on treasure guard, would protect him. Captains Orr and Thurburn spent the night at my house in the city.

During the night, the guards on duty in the city left their posts; towards morning various alarming reports were brought in, and I sent Mr. Bradford a note (which never reached him) requesting him to join us immediately. The city is a mile and a half from cantonments. All communication had been cut off, but we suspected what had happened, and our suspicions

* Note by Captain Hutchinson:—"This moulvie was lately killed near Mitholee, on the Shahjehanpore frontier."

were soon confirmed. A little after sunrise the mutineers—artillery, cavalry, and infantry—moved down upon the city; and, as we had no means of resistance, we were compelled to seek safety in flight.

As we rode off, I gave out that we were going to Shahgunj, and such was our original intention; but a little reflection convinced me that, with so many sowars thirsting for blood, it would be dangerous to attempt a road where we were certain to be pursued, if not, indeed, forestalled.

As soon, therefore, as we got out of sight, I turned off in another direction, and, after riding twelve miles, we entered a village called Goura, of which I knew the zemindars well. We were very kindly received, and, having sent intelligence of our safety to Shahgunj, we remained here till dark, when, as so many people had seen us approaching Goura, they thought it advisable to remove us to a solitary building two miles off, occupied by a pundit, a very fine old man, who had agreed to take us in.

While here, a sepoy of my regiment (late 37th) passed by and told the pundit that the native troops at Benares had been disarmed, and then massacred by artillery and a regiment of European infantry; that, afterwards, the Rajah of Benares, who was in league with the native troops, had come with a great host and killed every European in the place. The pundit repeated this to us, but, on being questioned, admitted that the sepoy appeared to have come in a great hurry; that he had no money, only his musket and regimental pantaloons, and was altogether in a miserable plight. This fully convinced us that the sepoy's story was false; but we failed to persuade the pundit that, had his ally won the day, the sepoy would not have beat so rapid a retreat or have come away empty-handed; neither could we undeceive him regarding the disarming and massacring at Benares.

The disarming and massacring story, which was industriously promulgated all over the country, was almost universally believed, and may have had most injurious effect. A native, in whom I placed considerable reliance, assured me that it was the immediate cause of the mutiny and cruel murders at Allahabad. The news of the capture by the mutineers of the fort of Allahabad was also circulated through Oude, and even we believed it for a time.

On the night of the 10th, the zemindars of Goura, who were most friendly and forward in their offers of assistance, came and escorted us, partly disguised, to Shahgunj. I would earnestly solicit that a suitable reward be granted to the pundit above mentioned, and to Baireesal and Juskura Sing, lumberdars of Goura, for their good service, which was the more meritorious, as they all shared in the common belief that our expulsion was final. The pundit even went so far as to predict that we should be succeeded by a "king from the west."

At Shahgunj we found Mr. Bradford, who had escaped from the city with some difficulty, owing, he believed, to the attempts of the criminal and revenue serishtadar to cause his destruction, and had reached Shahgunj on the 9th in disguise on foot, having been unable to get to the horse I had left for him. Subsequent information proved that the criminal serishtadar was not implicated in the attempt on Mr. Bradford.

The officiating head clerk, Mr. Martindell, with his son and two daughters, took refuge in the Waseeka buildings. Every one supposed the mutineers would respect these buildings, as females of the royal family resided in them; however, they were broken into, and all the money carried off, though I have been told it was afterwards returned. They robbed Mr. Martindell, and took him and his family prisoners. Of their fate I am quite uncertain, but fear the worst. As far as I know, they were not murdered at Fyzabad.

We had calculated on remaining at Shahgunj, as Maun Sing assured us he had no immediate apprehension of attacks, and that, during the rainy season, just about to set in, the fort, surrounded by low ground, was almost unapproachable.

The very morning, however, after our arrival, Maun Sing, who was at Adjoodheea, sent to say that the mutineers had promised not to molest the women and children, but insisted on his delivering up all the officers; and that, as he was not prepared to resist, and they threatened to search the fort the next day, we must prepare for instant departure, and that we should start, as soon as it was dark, for a ghaut on the Ghogra, where he would have boats waiting for us.

In the evening, I distributed a thousand rupees among the officers of the party; and, the arrangements having been completed, we got off a boat at 11 P.M., escorted by a party of doalbunds, and travelled across country as rapidly as possible, hoping to embark before daybreak; but the wheeled vehicles were much delayed by the difficulties of the route, and morning dawned long before we had reached the river.

Our situation was now very critical. With such a numerous party concealment was out of the question, and we were in broad daylight within seven or eight miles of Fyzabad, which was swarming with mutinous sowars, who, we knew, would have been only too glad of an opportunity to murder every one of us.

As we approached the river, a false alarm was given, and one or two shots were fired, which increased our uneasiness, but we reached the boats without any opposition; there we were greatly distressed to find that the carriage with the staff-sergeants' wives and children had broken down close to Shahgunj, and they had been obliged to return to the fort.

To have waited and sent back for them would most undoubtedly have occasioned the destruction of the whole party;

we believed, too, that our departure, which must become known to the troops in two or three hours, would prevent the threatened search of Shahgunj. After, therefore, repeatedly exacting from Maun Sing's karinda the most solemn promises (which were faithfully kept) that they should be protected, we embarked and pushed off.

The party consisted of the following persons:—Captain Reid, deputy commissioner, wife and two children; Captain Orr, assistant commissioner, wife and five children, and sister-in-law; Captain Thurburn, special assistant commissioner, wife and child; Mr. Bradford, extra assistant commissioner, and wife; Captain Dawson, executive engineer, wife and four children; Corporal Hurst, Sappers, wife and child; Mr. Fitzgerald, Nazool writer, wife and child—twenty-nine in all.

We were accompanied by a karinda of Maun Sing's and thirty doalbunds, who were never of the slightest use, but invariably disappeared on the slightest approach of danger.

The prevailing wind of the season is easterly, but fortunately on that day it was from the west, and we made rapid progress on our downward voyage. We kept out of sight as far as possible, and beyond occasional challenges from villages on the banks, no notice was taken of us till about midnight, when a boat came off with four or five armed men, making a great noise and uttering threats. Some of our party, who were nearest, were going to shoot these men, but I called out not to fire unless they attempted to come on board. They changed their tone as soon as they saw who we were, and asked for two or three rupees, which we gave, and they went off.

We proceeded without further molestation for two or three hours, when another boat came off, and the karinda went to meet it, all of us remaining concealed: he told us the men in the boat were retainers of Baboo Madhopershad of Birhur, who was a friend of Maun Sing, and for whom he had brought a letter recommending us to his care. We were not altogether satisfied, but did not oppose his taking our boat to the bank, in compliance with their request, at a fort called Nouruhnee.

On looking out, I saw there were two forts, thirty or forty yards distant, and that we were moored between them, right under the fire of both. Still, though uneasy, we did not become alarmed, till not only the karinda and his doalbunds walked off, but the boatmen, each with his little bundle, followed their example.

Shortly after, several armed men approached very close. I went out and spoke to them, threatening them with the anger of Maun Sing and Madhopershad if they molested us; but they paid very little heed to my threats; their numbers continued to increase, and their demeanour to become more and more violent, till we had every reason to fear the worst. We were evidently in extreme danger; and, as a last resource, Captain Orr and I went into one of the forts to see the leader of the ruffians, Ooditnarayun. I tried to frighten him, but at once saw the attempt was fruitless: he said he did not wish to murder us, but must have our arms, money, and valuables.

Two of our party had guns, and most of us had revolvers, without the means of reloading them; but, situated as we were, with eight ladies and fourteen children in an unwieldy boat quite immoveable, owing to the absence of the boatmen, and the head wind then blowing, and immediately under the fire of the two forts, resistance was hopeless, and we had no alternative but to accept the conditions, hard as they were. The robbers showed so much respect for us, that they did not attempt to enter the boat, but took the things as they were handed out to them.

Our boatmen now returned, and we attempted to proceed, but the head wind was so strong, that the boat was quite unmanageable; and, after whirling round once or twice, stuck fast. We spent there a most miserable day, feeling by no means safe from attack, and the sufferings of the ladies and children aggravated by the pangs of hunger.

About midday, a sepoy of my late regiment came to the boat. He affirmed he had been on leave when the corps mutinied; if not, he must have gone to his home immediately after. He appeared to be much affected, and said he would go and fetch Madhopershad, the baboo above referred to.

The sepoy never returned, but at sunset Madhopershad made his appearance, and promised to do everything in his power for us. He also sent us food, which was very acceptable. The wind having now somewhat abated, we started, but towards morning moored again, having made very little progress. A large party of sepoys with their arms passed us here in a fast boat. Our boatmen and theirs interchanged inquiries, but they appeared not to know who we were, and pulled steadily on. The sepoys were said to be bound for Azimghur.

After some hours' halt, we went on to a considerable village called Chihora, belonging to Madhopershad, where we remained five or six days, till we could make arrangements with some of his clan farther down the river, with whom he was at feud, for our proceeding unmolested.

We were quartered here in a sunken fort, in which was a small shed with a very thin thatched roof. The heat was most trying, and most of the ladies and all of the children were attacked by ophthalmia, from which their sufferings, which we had no means of alleviating, were most acute and protracted.

Our departure was put off from day to day, and it was not till the 19th June that we started for Gopalpore, which we reached, without further adventure, by midday of the 21st.

The marked loyalty of the Rajah of Gopalpore, as well as the aid which he rendered to several parties of fugitives, are well known to Government. We were here comparatively safe, and made our way by water, without difficulty, to Dinapore, where we arrived on the 29th June.

The following account by Sergeant-Major Busher will be read with much interest:—

On the morning of the 8th of June, news was brought into the station that the 17th Regiment Native Infantry, mutineers of Azimghur, were encamped a day's journey from Fyzabad, and intended marching into the station the following morning.

I received orders from Major Mills, commanding the battery, to send my family without delay to Shahgunj, and leave them under the protection of Rajah Maun Sing of that place. I accordingly did so, sending along with them the families of four other non-commissioned officers. In the evening, by order of Colonel Lennox, commanding the station, two companies of the 22nd Native Infantry were ordered to support our guns and to take up their position, one on either side of the battery, or a company on each flank: this they did. The officers and men, both Europeans and natives, remained with their guns all ready for action, when about 11 o'clock P.M. the alarm was sounded in the lines of the 6th Oude Irregular Infantry; on hearing which, the golundaz, or native artillerymen, immediately loaded their guns with grape. Whilst the port-firemen were in the act of lighting their port-fires, two companies of the 22nd Regiment that were placed on either side of the guns, rushed in, with loaded muskets in hand, amongst the artillery, and pointed them at the heads of the golundaz. Colonel Lennox, and the other officers of the 22nd Regiment, were on the spot almost immediately after the occurrence, and tried by every persuasion to get their men from the guns, but to no purpose. About this time, the whole of the 22nd Regiment left their lines and advanced towards our position, shouting. On coming up, they ordered us (the Europeans) to quit the place, and said the guns were no longer ours, but theirs. We were then escorted by a portion of the 22nd to the quarter guard of that regiment, and kept there under restraint till the following morning, when at break of day we were escorted to the river side, and directed to enter some boats that had been provided for us by the insurgents, and proceed down the river.

Whilst at the ghaut, intelligence was brought to our escort that the mutineers were helping themselves to the treasure. This caused the escort to hasten back to the lines as quickly as possible. Here I will take the liberty to mention that the rissaldar of the 5th Troop 15th Irregular Cavalry appeared to be the moving man in the mutiny, and undertook the general direction of affairs.

When the escort left us, we took to the boats—four in number—but found them without boatmen. However, as there was no time to proceed in search of boatmen, it was resolved that the boats should be manned by ourselves; so we got in, and, as far as my memory serves me, in the following order:—

In No. 1, or the First Boat.

1. Colonel Goldney, Commissioner.
2. Lieutenant Currie, Artillery.
3. Lieutenant Cautley, 22nd Regiment Native Infantry.
4. Lieutenant Ritchie, 22nd Regiment Native Infantry.
5. Lieutenant Parsons, 6th Oude Irregular Infantry.
6. Sergeant-Major Matthews, 6th Oude Irregular Infantry.
7. Sergeant Edwards, 13th Light Field Battery.
8. Sergeant Busher, 13th Light Field Battery.

IN NO. 2, OR SECOND BOAT.

1. Major Mill, Commanding 13th Light Field Battery.
2. Adjutant Bright, 22nd Regiment Native Infantry.
3. Sergeant-Major Hulme, 22nd Regiment NativeInfantry.
4. Mrs. Hulme.
5. Quartermaster-Sergeant Russel, 22nd Regiment Native Infantry.
6. Bugler Williamson, 13th Light Field Battery.

IN NO. 3, OR THIRD BOAT.

1. Colonel O'Brien, 6th Oude Irregular Infantry.
2. Captain Gordon, 6th Oude Irregular Infantry.
3. Assistant-Surgeon Collison, 6th Oude Irregular Infantry.
4. Lieutenant Anderson, 22nd Regiment Native Infantry.
5. Lieutenant Percivall, 13th Light Field Battery.

IN NO. 4, OR FOURTH BOAT.

1. Lieutenant Thomas, 22nd Regiment Native Infantry.
2. Lieutenant Lindesay, 22nd Regiment Native Infantry.
3. Lieutenant English, 22nd Regiment Native Infantry.

In the above order, we dropped down the river, on the 9th, a little before sunrise. Whilst dropping down, a sepoy of the 22nd Regiment, Teg Ally Khan, who had not joined the mutineers, was observed following in a canoe. He hailed, and requested to be taken with the party. He was accordingly taken in No. 1 boat. An hour or so after he was taken up, he made himself useful in procuring boatmen for Nos. 1 and 2 boats, near a village.

After a little delay, which proceeded from getting boatmen, we again proceeded, and in a short time, Nos. 1 and 2 passed the town of Adjoodheea. This was between 8 and 9 A.M. Boat No. 3 was observed to put in at Adjoodheea, and No. 4 was lost sight of, having dropped far astern.

Nos. 1 and 2 proceeded on, and, after leaving Adjoodheea about three miles in rear, put to, to await the arrival of Nos. 3 and 4. After waiting two hours, and seeing no signs of the boats coming, we again proceeded on for about nine coss, or eighteen miles, down stream, when we observed what appeared to us to be scouts running along the right bank of the river, and giving notice of our approach. We then suspected all was not right, that we had been duped, and purposely led into danger. On proceeding a little farther, we distinctly observed a regiment of mounted cavalry, and another of native infantry, in a body, at the narrowest part of the stream, awaiting our approach. We had no alternative but to proceed. When Nos. 1 and 2 boats arrived opposite to them, they opened a brisk fire on us. Sergeant Matthews, who was one of the rowers, was the first who fell, a ball having struck him at the back of his head; another ball struck my hat and knocked it into the stream, I myself sustaining no injury. Those in No. 2 boat, about 100 yards behind, seeing our hazardous situation, put their boats to at a sand-bank entirely surrounded by water. We, in No. 1 boat, then put to also and went ashore, when Colonel Goldney requested us to lay down our arms, and wait to see if we could come to terms with the mutineers, they directing their fire on us, Nos. 1 and 2, the whole time. Some boats with mutineers pushed off from the opposite shore and came towards us; when about the centre of the stream, they opened fire. Colonel Goldney, observing this, directed that those who could run, should, without any further loss of time, endeavour to escape, remarking that there was not even the shadow of a chance of our meeting with mercy at their hands, and at the same time added that he was too old himself to run. We now, seven in number, including Teg Ally Khan, took Colonel Goldney's advice, and gave leg bail, taking a direction across the country. I may here mention that from this period we remained in ignorance of the fate of Colonel Goldney and those of No. 2 boat. We now started and continued running, but did not do so long before meeting with an obstacle which precluded our further advance in the direction we marked out, and this was the junction of two streams of considerable width. Whilst at a standstill, and deliberating as to our future course, we saw a number of men coming towards us, whom we took for sepoys. All but Teg Ally Khan and Sergeant Edwards jumped into the stream and thought to escape by swimming to the opposite bank. After swimming a short distance, Teg Ally called out and told us to return, as they were only villagers. I, Lieutenant Ritchie, and Lieutenant Cautley returned, but Lieutenant Currie and Lieutenant Parsons got too far into the stream, and, in endeavouring to return were both, I regret to say, drowned. I myself narrowly escaped, having twice gone down, but, through the timely aid of one of the villagers, was safely got out. We had no sooner got out of the water, than we were again alarmed at seeing a boat full of people rounding a point, and thought they too were sepoys. We now ran and continued our course along the bank, not missing sight of the stream, until we were fairly exhausted. We then entered a patch of high grass growing at the riverside, or at a short distance from it, and rested ourselves. We missed Teg Ally Khan at this time. Whilst in our place of concealment, a boy herding cattle caught sight of us and ran towards the river, and with his herd crossed over, himself holding on by a buffalo's tail. On crossing over, it appeared, he informed the jemadar of the village of our situation; for, shortly after, the jemadar came down and called out to us, and told us not to be alarmed, and that he would bring a boat for us. This he did, and, on reaching his side of the river, he informed us that Teg Ally Khan had reported all particulars to him, and requested that a party might be sent in search of us, and that the boy who had been herding cattle brought him information of where we were. This jemadar very kindly took us to his hut, and entertained us as hospitably as he could, supplying us with provisions and cots to lie on; we remained under his protection till twelve o'clock, and, as we had the light of the moon, we commenced our journey and took the road for Amorah, the jemadar himself accompanying us to the next village; a little before entering which, we were surrounded by a party of freebooters, who demanded money. We told them we had none; but this did not serve them, and they satisfied themselves by searching our persons. When satisfied we possessed nothing, they offered no molestation, but allowed us to prosecute our journey. On entering the village, the jemadar who accompanied us made us over to a chowkedar, and directed him to take us to the next village, and make us over to the chowkedar of it; and thus we proceeded on from village to village, till we arrived at Amorah. Here we were rejoiced to meet the party that belonged to No. 4 boat, who told us that, as they could not get their boat along, they deserted her and proceeded across country. We were glad to find these gentlemen had arms, for we, who had joined them, had not even a stick. I must not forget to mention that Teg Ally Khan again formed one of our party, for we lost sight of him before crossing the river, where we experienced the kind treatment at the village jemadar's hands. We did not remain more than a few minutes at Amorah, as we were anxious to renew our journey. The tuhseeldar, who at this place gave us protection, further aided us by giving each a couple of rupees, and one pony to Lieutenant Ritchie, and another to Lieutenant Cautley, for the journey. We again started (now at 7 A.M. of the 10th), taking the road to Captain Gunje, under the guidance of a couple of thannah burkundazes.

We reached Captain Gunje safely, and inquired at the tuhseeldaree if there were any European residents at Bhustee, a place of some note, and were informed by the jemadar that there were not, but were told that he had received information that a party of the 17th Native Infantry, with treasure, had marched from Goruckpore *en route* to Fyzabad, and had halted at Bhustee, and advised us not to take the road to Bhustee, but to go to Gye ghaut, where he said we should meet with protection, and get boats to take us to Dinapore. The jemadar furnished us with five tattoos and fifty rupees, and put us under the protection of three burkundazes, giving them directions to proceed with us to Gye ghaut. We accordingly started, and after making about eight miles, sighted a village (Mohadubbah) which one of the burkundazes invited us to go to, telling us that we could rest ourselves there for a short time, and that he would refresh us with sherbet; we agreed, and this burkundaze who gave the invitation started off ahead, with the pretence of getting ready a place of accommodation and the sherbet. Nothing doubting that all was right, we proceeded on, as we thought in perfect safety. On nearing the village, the burkundaze again joined us, and had some conversation apart with the other two men. On our reaching it we observed, to our horror, that the whole village was armed; however, we made no remark, but passed on through it under the guidance of the three burkundazes. On getting to the end of it, we had to cross a nullah waist deep in the water; whilst crossing this, the villagers rushed upon us, tulwar and matchlock in hand. Seeing that they were bent on our destruction, we pushed through the water as quickly as possible, not, however, without leaving one of our number behind, who unfortunately was the last, and him (Lieutenant Lindesay) they cut to pieces. On reaching the opposite bank the villagers made a furious attack on us, literally butchering five of our party.

I and Lieutenant Cautley then ran, and most of the mob in

full chase after us. Lieutenant Cautley, after running about 300 yards, declared he could run no longer, and stopped; on the mob reaching him, he also was cut to pieces. After despatching poor Lieutenant Cautley, they continued the chase after me, but after running a short distance, and finding that I was a long way off, they desisted. I was now the only one left, not having even Teg Ally Khan with me. I proceeded, and in a short time came to a village, and the first I met was a Brahmin, of whom I begged a drink of water, telling him I was exhausted. He asked me where I came from, and what had happened to me. I told my tale as quickly as I could, and he appeared to compassionate my case. He assured me that no harm would come to me in his village, and that, as the villagers were all Brahmins, others would not dare to enter it to do me harm. He then directed me to be seated under a shady tree in the village, and left me; after a short absence he returned, bringing with him a large bowl of sherbet; this I drank greedily, and was hardly done, when he started up and bid me run for my life, as Baboo Bully Sing was approaching the village. I got up and attempted to run, but found I could not, so walked. I tried to get to some hiding-place: in going through a lane I met an old woman, and she pointed out an empty hut, and bid me run into it; I did so, and finding in it a quantity of straw, I laid down and thought to conceal myself in it. I was not long there, when some of Bully Sing's men entered and commenced a search, and used their lances and tulwars in probing into the straw; of course it was not long before I was discovered. I was dragged out by the hair of my head, and exhibited to the view of the natives who had congregated round him, when all sorts of abusive epithets were applied to me; and then commenced a march, leading me from village to village, exhibiting me, and the rabble at my heels hooting and abusing me. After passing through each, his men used to stop and tell me to kneel, and then ask Bully Sing if they were to decapitate me. His usual reply was, "Not yet; take him on to the next village." I was led into the court-yard and put in the stocks; this was about nightfall. During the night I heard angry words pass between Bully Sing and his brother; I could not exactly make out the particulars, but I remember his brother telling him to beware of what he was doing, and that his acts of the day would, perhaps, recoil upon himself. However, the result of the quarrel proved every way beneficial to me, for about three o'clock in the morning Bully Sing came to me himself, and directed my release from the stocks, and asked me if I should not like to have something to eat and drink, and his bearing towards me was entirely changed, and wholly different from what it had been.

The following morning a party made their appearance, headed by a villain, named Jaffir Ally, whom I recognized as the person who shot poor Lieutenant Ritchie the previous day, and who fired at me. Of this he made a boast at Bully Sing's when he saw me, and asked Bully Sing to make me over to him, and that he would burn me alive. He was told in reply, that I should be delivered over to no person, and to quit the place. This rascal then said my *kismut* was very good. I remained at Bully Sing's ten days, during which time I had no reason to complain of the treatment received; but this I mainly attribute to the interference of his brother in my behalf.

On the tenth day, a Mr. Peppy sent a darogha, with an elephant and an escort, to take me to him. I was glad of the opportunity, and willingly accompanied the party; but it was not without some trouble, and a good deal of persuasion, that the darogha induced Bully Sing to let me go. Anterior to this, a Mr. Cook, indigo planter, and Mr. Paterson, collector of Goruckpore, made several attempts to get me away from

Bully Sing, but to no purpose. I here offer my best and grateful acknowledgments to all three gentlemen for their kind consideration and endeavours on my behalf. On joining Mr. Peppy, I proceeded with him to Captain Gunje, and there, to my joy, I met Colonel Lennox and his family. Here we remained for the remainder of the day and night. The next morning, I accompanied Colonel Lennox to Bhustee, escorted by a party of sowars; here we were most hospitably entertained by Mr. Osburne, of the opium department. I shall not soon forget this gentleman's kindness, nor that of Colonel Lennox to me, and here offer to both my hearty and sincere thanks.

At Bhustee, we were joined by Teg Ally Khan, who managed to effect his escape from the onslaught at Mohadubbah. At Bhustee, we halted two days, and in the evening proceeded to Goruckpore, thence to Azimghur, and from Azimghur to Ghazeepore, without anything further of note occurring. At this station I arrived on the morning of the 26th June, thankful to Providence for bringing me safely through all my difficulties.

Next on the list is the mutiny at Selone, on the 9th of June, which is described as follows by Major Barrow, formerly deputy commissioner of that district:—

Up to the 1st June, the district was not much affected by the mutinies, and judging by the collections which were then going on for the rubbee kists, the talookdars and large zemindars had at this time no intention whatever of joining in rebellion, for without exception they paid up.

On the morning of the 8th June, I received positive intelligence from the deputy commissioner, Sultanpore, that mutinous troops were marching on Selone, Sultanpore, and Fyzabad. Probably these reports were made to the deputy commissioner to cause a panic, for on the same day the troops at that station mutinied. I attached no importance to this or other reports which were constantly being made, evidently with a view to get rid of us.

On the night of the 8th, Captain Thompson's regiment, the 1st Oude, requested permission to have their arms with them in case of an attack.

On the morning of the 9th, reports were made to me that both the Sultanpore and Fyzabad regiments had mutinied. A troop of Captain Harding's rissalah arrived at Selone without any orders. The rissaldar stated that the Sultanpore officers had fled through Pertabghur, and that place being abandoned, he had come to Selone. I discovered that some of his party had been engaged in the plunder at Purtabghur, and that others were fugitive sowars from Allahabad, where a portion of the regiment was stationed.

During the day, whilst at kutcherry, for the usual appearances were still kept up, and I had every confidence in the 1st Oude Regiment, several police fugitives and others arrived from Sultanpore and Purtabghur, two officers' horses were brought in, and several gaol fugitives from Allahabad were caught on the 8th and 9th.

About 1 P.M. of the 9th, some sowars came in and reported that the troops from Allahabad were *en route*, and another party intimated the troops from Sultanpore were at Attayah, about eight miles off: both reports no doubt were spread to create a panic.

I proceeded to the officer commanding, who had already given orders for his regiment to turn out. I accompanied him to the parade, and sent off parties of sowars in the directions intimated. After about two hours, nothing further occurring,

Captain Thompson ordered his men to pile arms. On being ordered to reassemble, they paid no attention. It was evident they intended to mutiny, but we took no notice whatever; extra sentries were put on, and the men were still under some control.

I paraded the troops of cavalry which had no European officer, and in reply to my address, they one and all declared they were faithful and would stand by me. The rissaldar privately told me, out of the eighty-five men, he could only depend on twenty.

All the officers assembled this night at my house. My wife and two children were the only officer's family present; there were the wives and children of two sergeants and one apothecary, besides the writers of my office.

The night passed quietly. Early in the morning I proceeded round the station, and observed the men of the Oude regiment carrying off their property to the neighbouring villages.

About 6 o'clock A.M., the guard of the gaol released the prisoners. Captain Thompson still thought he could bring his regiment round, and I determined to hold on as long as possible, but they clearly intimated at last that we had better leave; if we did not, they would not answer for our lives. No native officer even would now obey his call, and the regiment would furnish no guards for our protection.

At 2 P.M. my house was surrounded by all the budmashes of the place, including several of my own police, Passees, &c., clamouring for pay; they crowded close round it and looked hostile. I got out where the sowars were stationed, and induced twenty of them to mount and come to my house, when throwing out a bag of rupees to get them away from the verandahs, into which they had pressed, the sowars rode in between them and the house and drove them off, so far behaving well.

Whilst this was going on, preparations were made for the whole party to leave. A few sepoys of the regiment stated they would escort us through the lines (our course laying through them), but that they could not undertake to do so at a later period. The men, as we passed through, were all outside with their arms in their hands; some were respectful, others loaded their muskets as we passed them.

The sowars were on the right flank of the infantry, mounted, watching what was going on.

I was followed from the station only by my gaoler, with some twenty men and a private of the 33rd Regiment, with some fifty new levies; but ten of all ranks accompanied Captain Thompson. My police sowars and every one had deserted, with the above exceptions.

I had previously arranged with Humwunt Sing, of Kala Kunkur, that he should get together as many men as he could, and meet me the other side of the station; this he did, and escorted our whole party to his fort at Dharoopore, where we remained some fourteen days, when with the aid of other talookdars, the Thakorain of Bhudree and Sheodyal of Duheyaon, we succeeded in reaching Allahabad.

Baraitch.

Mr. Wingfield, the commissioner, thus describes the events at Baraitch:—

An untoward event occurred on the night of the 8th June which may have precipitated, by a few days, the final outbreak. Since the departure of the ladies all the remaining officers slept at my house, and four European sergeants kept watch by turns. About midnight we were awakened by two of the latter, who declared they had heard the men arming in the infantry lines, which were not above 250 yards from my house, and had even seen them forming up outside. They protested they had been close up to the lines; the night was very dark, and the view intercepted by trees. We could distinguish nothing, but believing the sergeants, went over to the encampment of the artillery, brought out the guns, and turned them on the lines of the infantry. No advance was made from that direction, nor was any movement discernible there. At the expiration of half an hour we returned to the house. I believe it was a false alarm, but there are officers who hold the contrary. I cannot forbear observing that on this occasion the best spirit appeared to be evinced by the artillery.

However that may be, it brought matters to a crisis. The sepoys declared we had tried to murder them in their sleep, and only been prevented by the refusal of the artillerymen to become the instruments of our cruelty. Heretofore there had been a coldness between the two arms, now they fraternized warmly. Captain Boileau sent for his native officers in the hope of explaining matters to them, but soon found he had lost all authority, and had to endure severe lectures and animadversions on his conduct from some of them who affected to be the spokesmen of the sepoys. Finally they dictated their own terms, and a parade of the regiment was ordered for that evening.

This took place in my house. Some old servants, who had been with me ever since I had been in India, had that day, and the previous one, told me that some of them had been warned to quit me, or they might lose their lives; and now Captain Boileau came and told me he no longer commanded the troops, and that he was going on parade in compliance with the intention he had expressed to that effect, but did not expect to leave it alive.

So evident was it for some time past that the troops were fast hurrying into revolt, that I would have left Secrora, which was not a civil station, or my legitimate place of residence, for Gonda before, had not Captain Boileau urged me to remain, alleging that my departure would show want of confidence in them. I now saw that my remaining any longer would be imperiling my own life, and therefore, taking the advantage of the habit of an evening ride, mounted my horse and rode over to Gonda, distant eighteen miles, where the 3rd Oude Irregular Infantry apparently remained loyal. Sir H. Lawrence had previously written to Captain Boileau and myself in these words,—"Should a mutiny break out, or appear inevitable, you are at liberty to consult your own safety." It had broken out. The troops had thrown off all authority, and the question was, how long they would leave us alive. In the lines (for they refused to parade that evening), Captain Boileau and his adjutant were grossly insulted by their men, who broke open the magazine, and conducted themselves in the most insubordinate manner. But their lives were not attempted. During the night, however, the house in which they slept was surrounded by the soldiery, who used threatening gestures, and kept them close prisoners till the following morning, when, profiting by the interval between the departure of the night guard and the arrival of the relief, they mounted their horses and rode away to Gonda and Bulrampore. The artillery officer, Lieutenant Bonham, who had slept in his battery, remained till 9 A.M., when he was expelled by his own men; he then took the road to Lucknow, which he reached in safety.

I will now describe the course of events at Gonda to the date of my arrival there. There, too, the attitude of the troops, consisting of the 3rd Oude Irregular Infantry, remained unaltered, and the civil business went on as usual; no falling off in the number of petitioners and other attendants in the court was noticeable till the beginning of June, when it was manifest that confidence in our power was fast departing, and zemindars who had recovered their villages from talookdars at settlement, were writing to propitiate the latter, or making preparations for flight. The tuhseeldars had reported that the sepoys had been overheard to express their determination not to allow the treasure, which there had been some talk of sending to Lucknow, to be removed; but the officers would not believe this, and certainly the behaviour of the men was most exemplary to the eye. Though I did not believe it possible they could withstand the force of example so close to them, still less soldiers who had lately served the king of Oude, I suffered Captain Mills to introduce his officers to me, when I told them what had occurred at Secrora, and listened to their professions of loyalty, and of determination to oppose the mutineers. I told them that the best proof of their loyalty would be to take the treasure and march with us to Bulrampore, or beyond the Raptee, for it was impossible they could oppose the Secrora mutineers, who, equally strong in infantry, had a horse field battery, and 150 cavalry besides. At first they agreed to this plan with seeming alacrity, but soon began to raise objections.

That night I passed at Gonda, as also the whole of the 10th. In the course of the day I received a hurried note from Lieutenant Bonham, to the effect that the troops at Secrora meant to march on Gonda, and force the regiment there to join them. We knew several letters had been received by the latter, and it soon became evident that no reliance was to be placed on this corps, and that it would do as its brethren in arms had done.*

* Captain Hutchinson notes here that he ascertained from Lieutenant Bonham himself that he remained at Secrora with his two

Having objected to the plan of going to Bulrampore, on some frivolous pretext, they said they would stay and fight the mutineers, and when driven from that subterfuge, next said they would march into Lucknow with the treasure and European officers.

Just at this time a letter came to us from Lieutenant Clarke, commanding a detachment of the regiment at Baraitch, showing the state of disaffection that prevailed in it; and news of the mutiny at Fyzabad and flight of the European officers on the previous day arrived also. I felt satisfied that to stay any longer was to court destruction unprofitably; and, therefore, gave the civil officers permission to leave, and about 10 P.M., in company with Mr. Owen, assistant commissioner, and two officers of the 2nd Oude Irregular Infantry, set out on horseback for Bulrampore. Captain Mills and his adjutant thought themselves bound by a sense of duty to remain till their men openly renounced their authority, for, though determined to do only what pleased them, their attitude was as yet respectful, and Lieutenant E. Clarke, assistant commissioner, determined to stay with these officers.

We reached Bulrampore without hindrance next morning the 11th, and not many hours afterwards were joined by the officers of the 3rd Regiment and Lieutenant Clarke. They had passed the night at Gonda, but at daybreak the havildar major showed them a letter from the Secrora mutineers to his corps, bidding it repair to Secrora with the treasure. He told them the regiment would join the rest, and urged them to make their escape while there was yet time. In this advice some of the

artillery sergeants after the infantry had mutinied and driven away all their officers, and that he only left when the infantry, some hours afterwards, rushing on the guns, drove him away, his men protecting him as long as they could. Both he and his sergeants reached Lucknow safely, wonderful to relate.

native officers joined, and even escorted their European officers through the cantonment.

At Bulrampore, Captain Boileau and all were most kindly and hospitably entertained by the Rajah, though it was not difficult to perceive our presence was not much liked by many of his followers. A letter was shortly afterwards received by him from the mutineers, desiring him to make over the treasure in the tuhseel; and the bearer, a sowar, reproached him with harbouring Europeans. It was evident our remaining there would bring him into trouble, and us into danger. There was no apparent prospect of the rains setting in; the mutineers could have marched with their guns in one night from Gonda, and the Rajah's house was not fortified. Nor could his people be depended on to protect us at the risk of their own lives. We accordingly determined on leaving; and, on the evening of the 12th, set out under escort of the Rajah and 500 of his men for Phoolpore, a place belonging to him, just within the borders of the Goruckpore district. At that time, we were uncertain whether Goruckpore was still in the hands of the British authorities; but our intention was, at all events, to proceed to Bansee, the Rajah of which place was a relative of the Rajah of Bulrampore; and there, if we found Goruckpore closed to us, to decide whether we should make for the Gunduck, and drop down that river to Patna, or seek an asylum in Nepaul. We halted this day at Phoolpore, and reached Bansee on the 14th.

Here we learnt the real posture of affairs at Goruckpore, which was critical enough; but the authorities had full confidence in the Irregular Cavalry, and Captain Boileau and the officers decided on going there, and on to Ghazeepore and Benares. I resolved to wait for further news from my division, for none of the talookdars had yet shown any indication of revolt; and I thought it probable that the mutinous troops would all march towards Lucknow, when I might, with the aid of the well-affected rajahs, return and re-establish the British authority. Besides, all communication from other parts had ceased since the 8th, and I was ignorant how far mutiny had spread in our older provinces, and they were equally so, for the same reason, at Goruckpore.

But a letter from the Rajah of Bulrampore soon showed me how useless it would be to return without British troops, and I therefore resolved to go on to Goruckpore, which I reached on the 26th.

Baraitch.

The daily bulletins of the deputy commissioner Mr. Cunliffe, represented that district as perfectly free from disorder or agitation, almost up to the very last communication that I received from him, which was dated the 7th or 8th. But he was alive to the impending danger, and had, as he fancied, secured himself and companions a safe retreat in Nanpara, that family having been treated with the greatest kindness by our officers, and been immensely benefited by the annexation. The Rajah was a minor under the Court of Wards, under the guardianship of his mother, and the agent and manager was one Kullun Khan, an old and trusted dependant of the family.

I counselled Mr. Cunliffe when the storm burst to seek the protection of Rajah Koolraj Sing, of Pudnaha, a hill Rajpoot with whom we had been intimate, but he trusted Kullun Khan, who had assured him a generous reception.

I have already said Lieutenant Clarke had become aware of the disaffected spirit of his men, but I cannot learn they had broken out into open mutiny when the European gentlemen decided on quitting the station. On the 10th, the Hissampore tuhseel of the Baraitch district had been plundered by a detachment of sepoys from Secrora, and the gentlemen must have heard of it when they left, which they did on the night of the 11th, reaching Nanpara, which is distant not more than twenty-five miles, on the following morning. Futtehshah Khan, extra assistant commissioner, accompanied them; the third European was Mr. Jorden, extra assistant commissioner.

There, instead of finding shelter, they met with the blackest treachery. They were denied even an hour's repose and a little food by Kullun Khan, who pretended that the Rajah of Churda, who resided close by, was coming after them, and I have heard that it was in consequence of intelligence that Kullun Khan had laid an ambush for them on that road, that instead of proceeding onward to Pudnaha or into the Terai, where they would have been safe among the Tharroos, and could have entered into Nepaul at any time, they decided on returning to Baraitch, which they reached after nightfall.

Then instead of proceeding to Bulrampore, where they knew I had repaired, and which they might have reached in safety, they resolved to make for Lucknow, but their horses being completely exhausted they purchased others from the mounted military police, and, disguising themselves as sowars in native attire, and with an escort of that corps, succeeded in reaching Byram Ghaut. The accounts differ as to how they met their death there, but Futtehshah Khan, the extra assistant commissioner, who was the only eye-witness from whom I have received any relation of the particulars, says, that no sooner had they got on board the boat, than the sowars took away their horses, which were to have followed in another; this attracted the observation of a party of the Secrora sepoys guarding the ghauts, who, on questioning the sowars, and learning the true character of their seeming companions, pursued them in boats and shot them in midstream. Mr. Jorden, he relates, was kept alive for some days, and put to death by order of the subadar commanding at Secrora.

Futtehshah Khan * escaped with his life, because he was a native, but after he was robbed of everything. He made his way to Setapore, and thence to Bareilly, where, I make little doubt, he has been deep in rebel counsels, though he has not openly taken office. But his brother and uncle were respectively nazims of Bareilly and Budaon under Khan Bahadoor, and he is an able, ambitious man and a bigot too.

There was only one European clerk at Baraitch, and he happened to be away on leave. When he arrived within a mile or two of Baraitch, on his return there, he heard the European officers had fled, and at once took the road to Bulrampore, which he reached while I was there.

DURRIABAD.

This station had participated in the general uneasiness felt in the neighbouring stations, but up to the 8th of June no open opposition to the British Government had occurred, perilling the lives of the Christian community.

* He was executed on the reoccupation of Rohilcund for a treasonable letter addressed by him to Waladad Khan, of Malaghur.

In May, the treasure had been ordered into Lucknow, but the sepoys, apparently, were not to be trusted, and the authorities feared hurrying them into revolt. Early in June great efforts were made to get the regiment there, the 5th Oude, to march with the treasure to Lucknow. On the evening of the 8th, the treasure was laden on carts and orders issued for marching. There is no reliable account of what immediately caused the outbreak, but it appears the Christian residents were apprized of it by the firing of musketry almost before the whole line of treasure carts had got out of the cantonments. The Europeans all managed to escape except two clerks, Messrs. Forbes and Wiltshire, who were taken prisoners by the sepoys, and after much insult and ill-treatment liberated. They managed to reach Lucknow safely, whither the principal civil and military officers and the larger portion of the Christian community also went.

GONDA.

Lieutenant Clarke, assistant commissioner, thus describes the mutiny at this station:—

On the 15th of June, about 3 P.M., I received a note from Mr. Wingfield, the commissioner of Baraitch Division, and who was residing at Secrora at the time, to the effect that all the ladies at that station were to start for Lucknow in the evening; and, therefore, the ladies of Gonda had better take advantage of the opportunity to be off and join the party, as, in all probability, no other opportunity would offer itself, and the road to Lucknow, in a day or two, would most assuredly be closed by the rebels.

The assistant-surgeon of the regiment, Dr. Bartrum, and myself being the only married officers in the place, we consulted with the officers of the corps as to whether, in their opinion, the sending away of the ladies would have a bad effect on their men or not; and, on receiving a reply in the negative, we determined to start immediately with our wives to Secrora. This we did, and reached that station about midnight, where, taking leave of our wives, and giving them over to the protection of a guard of Captain Boileau's regiment, the 2nd Oude Irregular Infantry, which was waiting in readiness to escort them to where the Secrora ladies had proceeded, we returned, next morning, to Gonda.

On receiving the note alluded to, the sergeant-major of the 3rd, and the married clerks of the deputy commissioner's office, when informed of the determination, came to beg Dr. Bartrum and myself to go to Secrora; and they were invited to take advantage of the same opportunity, but some circumstances or other, which I now forget, prevented their coming with us; so, a day or two afterwards, the married clerks were permitted to take their wives and families to Bulrampore. The wife and family of the sergeant-major also accompanied the party.

From the 6th to the 9th, all went as smoothly at Gonda as it had ever done before; when, on the evening of the latter date, we were all thrown into a state of anxiety by the arrival of Mr. Wingfield, who informed us that he had just ridden over from Secrora, as Captain Boileau's regiment was all but in open mutiny; he further informed us that the troops of Fyzabad had mutinied.

We were aware that the troops of Durriabad had already mutinied, and now that the Fyzabad and Secrora troops had followed their example all roads from the Gonda districts were closed. Captain Miles, therefore, immediately sent to the lines, summoned the native officers of his regiment, informed them of what Mr. Wingfield had told us, explained to them how all egress from the district, except *viâ* Bulrampore, was now closed, and suggested to them the advisability of the regiment marching off next morning, with all the money in the Gonda treasury, to Bulrampore, a small town about thirty miles off, and the residence of a friendly rajah. This plan they all agreed to at once, and immediately sent sepoys to procure carriage from the city and the surrounding villages, and by the next morning (the 10th instant) most of the carriages were in the lines ready for a start.

The information given us by Mr. Wingfield the preceding evening was painfully confirmed by the arrival, the next morning (10th inst.), at about 8 A.M., of Lieutenant Hall and Assistant-Surgeon Kendall, who rode in at full gallop, and told us that Captain Boileau's regiment, to which they belonged, had broken out into open mutiny, and that he (Captain Boileau), like themselves, had to flee for his life; but they added the gratifying intelligence that the men of Lieutenant Bonham's light field battery were still firm.

Writing as I do from memory, I am not quite certain why the plan of going to Bulrampore was not carried out the next morning, but I believe the causes were two: first, because of the intelligence given by Lieutenant Hall concerning the state of the artillery at Secrora, which was confirmed by a note from Lieutenant Bonham himself, about 12 A.M. of the same day; and, secondly, to enable the detachment of the 3rd Oude

Infantry, which was on command at Baraitch, to rejoin the regimental head-quarters, before they marched for Bulrampore; but, be the cause what it may, the proposed plan was not carried out.

On the evening of the 10th, we received another note from Lieutenant Bonham, in which he stated that, two hours after writing the first letter, he had been driven out of his battery, and was then on his way with one or two men to Lucknow, intending to cross the river Gogra at Gurkhoeea Ghaut. The note had evidently been written in a hurry, for it was but a scrap of paper, and in pencil.

Captain Miles again assembled his native officers and ordered them to prepare to march with the treasure to Bulrampore; but this time they demurred, made excuses, and at last coolly said they would go to their lines, and, after reflecting upon the matter, would give an answer in the course of a few hours. On hearing this answer, Mr. Wingfield and the others, who had come from Secrora, decided on leaving during the night for Bulrampore.

The few hours expired; the native officers returned. They reiterated their former excuses, and added a few fresh ones, but all to the same purport. Captain Miles explained to them that their excuses were absurd, as there was but one road open, and that was the one to Bulrampore. He argued with them and tried to bring them to a sense of their duty, warning them that their conduct was becoming sensibly mutinous.

Seeing that he could not prevail on them to do what was right, he dismissed them to their lines, directing a strong picquet to be sent to a nullah on the road between Gonda and Secrora, to give notice of the approach of any mutineers from the latter station. He then advised that all of us should sleep in the same house, in case of any outbreak on the part of the men during the night.

Concurring as we all did in the correctness of this advice, we had our beds brought into the open verandah of the adjutant's house, which was nearest to the lines and treasury. We remained half dressed, and had our horses ready saddled in the compound, in case of being obliged to run for it.

The night passed by without any molestation from the sepoys, but more than once a sepoy with a shouldered musket passed close to our beds (I suppose to see if we were there), and more than once we heard a hubbub in the lines; the picquet, also, which was sent out on the Secrora road, returned some time before they ought to have done, and when they came near the house where we were, the men tossed about their muskets and went into the lines in a most disorderly manner, laughing and talking boisterously.

At daybreak, the havildar major of the regiment brought Captain Miles a letter he had received during the night from the mutineers at Secrora, in which the men of the 3rd Regiment were urged to seize both the treasury and their officers. This determined Captain Miles to make one more effort to bring the native officers to reason, whereupon he summoned them once more, and again ordered them to march to Bulrampore, telling them that if they would not obey him he would leave them. They flatly refused to go to Bulrampore, and indeed anywhere. Captain Miles then sent for his two sergeants, and when they had joined us, we all mounted our horses and left the station, at a walking pace, making for Bulrampore, which we reached the same evening.

At the Rajah of Bulrampore's house we met Mr. Wingfield and others, and we remained there till the night of the 13th instant, when, starting about midnight, we reached, at about 10 P.M., a village by name Biscanah, which is in the Goruckpore district, and belongs to the Rajah of Bulrampore. Remaining there a day, we started in the night for the Rajah of Bhunsee's house, where, after remaining a few days, we went into the station of Goruckpore.

I consider I am here bound to record that the late lamented Sir Henry Lawrence, with his usual consideration and kindness, after the massacre at Setapore, sent round a circular to those commanding officers whose regiments in Oude had not as yet mutinied, telling them that if they found they could not keep their men quiet, but that the mutiny of their corps appeared inevitable, they had his permission to leave their regiment.

There is but little doubt that this permission was the means of saving the Europeans of the stations of Gonda and Secrora.

The following is a list of the names of those who received shelter and hospitality from Rajah Dirgbijey Singh, Rajah of Bulrampore:—

C. J. Wingfield, Esq., commissioner of Gonda, Baraitch Division.

C. B. Owen, Esq., officiating deputy commissioner of Gonda.

Lieutenant E. G. Clarke, assistant commissioner of Gonda.

Captain G. Boileau, commanding	2nd Oude Irregular Infantry.
Lieutenant G. Hale, adjutant	
B. Kendall, assistant-surgeon	
Captain C. Miles, commanding	3rd Oude Irregular Infantry.
Lieutenant D. Campbell, adjutant	
F. Bartrum, assistant-surgeon	
— Lynch, sergeant-major	
P. Carr, quartermaster-sergeant	

Mr. C. Tucker, head clerk, deputy commissioner's office, Gonda.

Mr. Yeoward, 2nd clerk, ditto, ditto.

Brother-in-law, wife and family of Mr. Tucker.

Family of Mr. Yeoward.

Wife and family of Sergeant-Major Lynch.

Mr. Archer, head clerk, deputy commissioner's office, Baraitch.
Another clerk, name unknown, but I think belonging to commissioner's office, Baraitch:—nineteen individuals, exclusive of children, the number of whom I do not now remember.

Sultanpore.

It appears from various accounts that the mutiny at this station was commenced on the 8th or 9th of June by the Military Police Regiment firing at the late Lieutenant-Colonel S. Fisher, whilst he rode past their lines after an interview with Mr. Block, the deputy commissioner.

Colonel Fisher, who commanded the 15th Irregular Cavalry, managed to reach his own lines, where he was met by his two officers, Captain A. Gibbings and Lieutenant C. W. Tucker. They succeeded with difficulty in getting him into a dooley. Feeling himself mortally wounded, he begged them to leave him and provide for their own safety.

Very soon the men of the regiment attacked them, killing Colonel Fisher and Captain Gibbings, but Lieutenant Tucker succeeded in escaping across country.

Captain Bunbury, commanding the police regiment there, and other officers, escaped to a friendly rajah, and the ladies were protected by the Rajah of

Ameatee, whither they had previously been sent for safety.

The deputy commissioner, Mr. Block, and Assistant Commissioner Stroyan, were both murdered on the opposite bank of the Goomtee; and the following deposition gives as authentic an account of the sad tragedy as can be procured :—

Deposition of Sheikh Emambux, late gaoler in the Sultanpore District of Oude, taken on the 3rd of September, 1858.

On the 10th of May, 1857, I was ordered by Mr. Block, deputy commissioner of Sultanpore, to proceed to Chandah (ten coss east of Sultanpore) with Luchmun Pershad, kotwal of Sultanpore, with a view of instituting inquiries regarding a quarrel that had lately taken place in the vicinity of Chandah amongst some zemindars. Whilst at Chandah, about the 5th of June, 1857, I received information that the troops at Jaunpore had mutinied, and had plundered the station, and that the mutineers had, shortly after the outbreak, been joined by troops from Benares. I immediately despatched an urzee to Mr. Block (on the 5th), informing that gentleman of what I had heard. I also sent spies towards Jaunpore, and, on their return, they informed me that the mutinous troops at Jaunpore, after having plundered the treasury, houses, &c., were marching towards Sultanpore. I again wrote to Mr. Block, and immediately collected all the chowkedars and gooraits of the neighbourhood, and ordered them to remain at the thanah and tuhseel at Chandah, both of which had been previously strengthened by a party of forty Rajkoomar Rajpoots, sent there by Mr. Block. These arrangements had hardly been made, when I heard that the insurgents had actually reached

Koeripore, which is about three miles east of Chandah. Not receiving, through the chowkedars whom I had sent out for information, correct accounts of the advance of the rebels, I determined upon going myself to Koeripore. On my arrival there, I saw 500 or 600 men, sepoys. They had evidently been marching in great haste; they wore their native clothes, and had converted their uniform broad-cloth pantaloons into bags, having filled them with rupees. They had their belts and muskets. The bunneahs at Koeripore had fled, and the sepoys succeeded with difficulty in obtaining sugar for sherbet, by paying one rupee per seer for it. As I was disguised as a common ryot, I easily mixed amongst them, and asked them if any other troops were coming in the same direction. They told me that a few more *would* join them, and that one regiment of infantry, and one of cavalry, had gone from Jaunpore towards *Fyzabad*, and one regiment of infantry towards Purtabghur, and they themselves were *en route* to Sultanpore. They also said that they had killed some officers at Jaunpore, taken possession of the treasury, &c.; adding that Benares and Allahabad were both in the hands of the sepoys, and that it was now the *Telinga Raj*. They said that the 8th Regiment Oude Irregular Force at Sultanpore had turned "Christian" (*i.e.* made use of the cartridges); but that the 1st Regiment Military Police, 15th Irregular Cavalry, were true to the cause. Hearing all this, I returned speedily to Chandah, and once more wrote to Mr. Block. This was the second urzee I had despatched this day (6th June) to Sultanpore.

I was now in hourly expectation of the arrival at Chandah of the rebel troops, and had sent spies to give immediate notice of their approach. One spy returned, after a long delay, and told me that the rebels at Koeripore had asked him how many men were at Chandah. The chowkedar answered that, taking into account chowkedars, gooraits, police, &c., there were at least 500 men at Chandah. They then gave him three rupees (which he showed me) to conduct them by an indirect road, so as to avoid Chandah, towards Sultanpore.

I again despatched this chowkedar with two or three others, and, on their return, was informed that the rebels had, on their arrival at a village three miles south of Chandah, separated into two parties; one party was to cross the Goomtee at Dhuppass Ghaut (about twenty miles east of Sultanpore), and the other party was to proceed towards Meerapore-Kuturat, eight miles south of Sultanpore. The spy could not discover the reasons for this separate move. I again forwarded this information to Sultanpore. On the 7th, I received a perwannah from Mr. Block, ordering me back to Sultanpore, as he was anxious that I should return to my post at the Sultanpore gaol. I waited a short time at Chandah to wait the arrival of a thanadar to whom to make over charge, and at about twelve o'clock I started for Sultanpore. On the road I heard the sound of musketry, and shortly afterwards I received information that a fresh body of rebel troops from Jaunpore had reached *Chandah*, and had completely plundered it. Farther on, near Lumbooah, which is fourteen miles south-east of Sultanpore, I saw large bodies of troops proceeding towards Sultanpore; these halted at Lumbooah. I continued my road, and reached Sultanpore at 4 o'clock P.M. Before reaching the station, I met successively several sepoys of the 8th Regiment Oude Irregular Force and of the military police, who each told me that things had gone wrong, and that on the following day (9th June) "whatever was to happen would happen" ("*jo kooch hona hai, hoga*"). I proceeded quickly to Mr. Stroyan's (assistant commissioner's) house, where I also found Mr. Block. Mr. Stroyan was ill and in bed. I now mentioned all that I had heard and seen. Mr. Block immediately wrote a note to Colonel Fisher, commanding Sultanpore, whose lines were at Badshahgunge, two miles from the station. He shortly arrived, and I was again told to repeat what I had already stated. Colonel Fisher asked whether I thought it would be advisable for him to take a body of horse and foot, and attack suddenly the rebels at Lumbooah? I at once answered that his own men could not be depended upon, and I again repeated what the sepoys had told me as I was approaching the station that morning. After a long consultation carried on in English, Colonel Fisher returned to his lines at Badshahgunge. After his departure, I begged of the gentlemen to leave the station, but they refused to do so. Early next morning, Colonel Fisher again came to the station, and, after speaking to the gentlemen, started in the direction of the cantonment of the military police, near Badshahgunge, where some disturbance had taken place: a short time after his departure, I heard the sound of musketry. I mounted one of the bastions of the gaol, and saw that the bungalows of the officers of the 15th Irregular Cavalry had been set on fire, and was soon told that Colonel Fisher had been killed by the men of the military police. I ran and gave notice of this to Messrs. Block and Stroyan, who at length made preparations for flight. By this time, some of the sepoys and sowars from Badshahgunge had entered the station. The two gentlemen, accompanied by a Hindoo writer boy and myself, walked towards the river which runs under Mr. Block's garden. Here Mr. Stroyan, who was, as already stated, ill, mounted Mr. Block's horse. We went along the river-side under the high bank, and crossed it a little to the eastward of Captain Bunbury's house. After crossing, we were guided by one Mowla Buksh, jemadar of Chuprassies, who, it appeared, promised Mr. Block to conceal him. He took us to a small house, close to the town of Sultanpore and to its eastward, near the river; it was a very small place. Arrived here, Mr. Block urgently asked me to return to the station and see what was going on there. I did so; and found that the prisoners had been released, the bungalows all in flames, and the property being plundered. I endeavoured to persuade Gungadeen, a jemadar of Chuprassies, with some of his men, to accompany me back to the spot where the gentlemen had taken refuge. I now returned to Sultanpore (town). On reaching the small house where I had left Mr. Block, I saw one Yaseen Khan, resident of Sultanpore, seated before the door—*and no one in the house.* I asked Yaseen Khan where the gentlemen were. He answered in a ferocious manner, abusing me at the same time. He would, doubtless, have murdered me, had not a friendly person, by name Soobhan Khan, made me a sign to move on. I did so; and, hiding as much as possible in the high grass, moved along the bank of the river, eastward. At a short distance, I met a boy of about ten years of age, who told me that the people of Sultanpore had murdered the gentlemen. I asked him to show me the place where the bodies were. He did so; and at about a mile from the town (to the north-east) I found them. The body of Mr. Block was in deep water; I saw the mark of a ball on his right temple. Mr. Stroyan's body was on the dry ground at some distance from the bank of the river: it was dreadfully marked with deep sword-cuts. He had evidently advanced from the river-side to face the enemy, one of whom he had succeeded in wounding. Whilst I was looking at the bodies, a Mahomedan zemindar came up to the spot, and I begged him to assist me in bringing Mr. Stroyan's body. He consented, and called out to some men working in a field hard by. With the assistance of these men, I dug the ground deep enough to admit of the body being placed within; I covered it with as much earth as circumstances would allow me to scrape together. I would also have buried Mr. Block's body; but, owing to the depth of the water in which it was floating, I could not reach it.

From the boy who had guided me, I learnt that Mowla Buksh, shortly after the arrival of the gentlemen in his house, cried out: "The people of Sultanpore are threatening to attack me, because I have given refuge to Europeans, but I shall defend them with my life." This ruse of the wretch succeeded, for on hearing this boast more than once repeated, Messrs. Block and Stroyan thought naturally that it would be advisable now to leave the place, which was no longer one of concealment. They consequently marched in an easterly direction along the bank of the river, which bank is excessively high and steep. They were soon followed by Mowla Buksh and others, running along the top of the bank and firing upon the fugitives. The latter were, however, protected by the high bank. At length, the bank slopes into the plain; and here, with nothing to protect them from the balls of the assassins, they soon fell. It would appear that Mr. Block, on receiving his first wound, rushed into the river, hoping to cross, but a second ball deprived him of life.

After burying Mr. Stroyan, I returned once more to Sultanpore (town), where I was kindly received by one Rujjub Khan, commandant, to whom I related what had happened. He abused Mowla Buksh, saying, that from his very birth he had been a "*dugga baz*" (full of deceit). I now crossed the river, and proceeded *viâ* Durriabad to Lucknow, which place I reached several days before the affair at Chinhut. My deposition was taken by Mr. Gubbins, financial commissioner.

Whilst the out-stations round Lucknow were thus falling one by one, and numerous fugitives daily reaching Lucknow, the most active preparations were in progress under the vigilant superintendence of the late Sir Henry Lawrence, K.C.B., to make a successful stand in Lucknow.

Sir Henry's vigilance was untiring: often did he rouse his secretary, Mr. Couper, and, attended by him alone, go out at night for hours, personally satisfying himself of the state of things around him in that large city, the perpetual cause of his anxiety and care.

It had first been hoped that our numbers would have been sufficient to hold both the fortified places, called the Muchee Bhawun and the Residency. The former was considered the key to Lucknow by all the country round; it was the old citadel of the sheikhs of Lucknow, who, when the seat of government was at Fyzabad, held here supreme authority.

It was therefore deemed desirable to maintain the show of holding this fort, whilst every arrangement was made for evacuating it when we should be so hard beset as not to have enough defenders for both places.

The following letter by Sir Henry Lawrence shows at once his clear and decided opinion on the subject. It was written when he held the cantonment before alluded to, and where Sir Henry then was, as we did not withdraw from thence till a later date.

The letter is addressed to General Sir John

Inglis, K.C.B., but then colonel and commanding in the Residency:—

MY DEAR INGLIS, *June* 11*th*, 1857.

Pray get me a big room, or two smaller rooms, sufficiently large to hold six or eight of us, in a *central* position, and where I shall not be *very hot.* It is important for me to be as cool as possible, as I feel the heat greatly. It is also necessary that I should be near the middle of our position. My staff, and you, and Anderson,* ought, I think, to be with me day and night. I am *decidedly* of opinion that we ought to have only *one* position, and that though we should hold all *three* cantonments and Muchee Bhawun as long as we can, all arrangements should be made with reference to a *sudden* concentration at the Residency.

1st. The treasure ought, therefore, to be removed to the Residency.

2nd. The grain be brought there.

3rd. The mortars and their ammunition.

4th. The mass of the powder and small-arm ammunition, &c.

5th. The eighteen-pounders: but the two in position should not be moved until they are replaced by two old guns, or suspicion will be excited.

6th. In short, as quickly though as quietly as possible, *all* the munitions and stores should be got into the Residency, and the nine-pounder field battery *only* with a few old guns in possession (to be spiked before abandoned) be left to accompany the troops at the last moment. The withdrawal will not be easy at any time; so the less that is left to bring away at the last moment the better.

* Sir Henry here referred to the late lamented Major Anderson, of the Bengal Engineers.

Pits should be *at once* dug here for the grain and powder. Every cart and waggon of batteries, as well as of the magazines, should be employed in bringing in stores; and Captain Carnegie should furnish hackeries for grain, and elephants to carry old guns, as many as possible of which ought to be brought.

Yours very sincerely,

(Signed) H. LAWRENCE.

P.S.—11th, 4 P.M. Please read this with Anderson, and consult with him as to the extension of the Residency works, so as to enable the whole force of seven hundred Europeans, and say as many natives of all sorts, and the work should be carried on *day* and *night*.—H. L.

In pursuance of these instructions and suggestions, Captain Fulton, the executive engineer, aided by Lieutenant Anderson, of the Madras Engineers, somewhat extended the Residency entrenchment, and by their judicious arrangements completed a fortification which turned every house to advantage, and secured as much flanking defence as possible.

All departments at this time, as may well be conceived, were working to their very utmost; Mr. Gubbins, the financial commissioner, I believe, took especial charge of the intelligence department, most important in those days; Mr. Ommaney, judicial commissioner's arrangements of that nature; whilst Major Banks, the commissioner of Lucknow, was indefatigably employed from morning till night in every possible kind of duty. Mr. Martin, the deputy commissioner, was all day on horseback, urging the sluggish bunneahs to send in their grain, and in this he was well aided by all below him; whilst Captain James, the commissariat officer, worked as if he had foreseen the long siege before him.

The civil authority and commissariat chiefly busied themselves in getting in stores, the artillery in bringing in our guns, destroying old ones, and labouring to stow away within our defences the enormous collection of old guns belonging to the former kings of Oude. Day and night carts were incessantly plying. Lieutenant Innes, the engineer officer of the Muchee Bhawun, had admirably completed his defences; but, as we have seen, their excellence was not to be proved. Demolitions of an immense number of houses were effected under Captain Fulton's orders all round the Residency; but when the siege commenced, vast numbers still remained. Some few days before the siege commenced, Sir Henry Lawrence walked round and viewed the demolitions: necessary as they were, he still felt for those thus dispossessed, and inquired from me with solicitude, if his express orders had been carried out, and all the houses registered and valued, so that compensation might be given.

Hundreds of men, women, and children were daily employed digging ditches, putting up stockades, and building batteries; but our position, necessarily extended, required more time and labour to complete its fortifications than were possible. The late Major Anderson, attended by Lieutenant Tulloch, his aide-de-camp, was constantly about, over the works, stimulating all by his advice and example. To work in those days needed no stimulus; had it been wanting, the affection borne to Major Anderson by all his subordinates would have more than supplied it. The Residency grounds at this time were very full. Most of the officers bivouacked in the open air entirely; and many will remember how interesting was the progress of the Redan Battery, which rose gradually under the eye of the late lamented Captain George Fulton, of the Engineers, one of the many thousand and one things by him all comprehended, all well done; when time had proved his excellence and value, he fell: all mourned his loss.

According to Sir Henry's orders, the treasure, twenty-seven lakhs, was removed from the Muchee Bhawun into the Residency; numerous pits dug to contain munitions of war; and grain, &c., stowed away in buildings, the church, amongst other places, being filled with supplies.

European merchants were allowed to bring in all their supplies, on condition of selling them at the same prices as before. Mr. Hill, of the firm of Thacker and Co., be it recorded to his honour, rigidly kept his promise, and when tea was a fabulous price per seer, sold it at the same rate as before. No furniture or carriage, &c., were allowed to be brought inside the entrenchment, only boxes containing wearing apparel.

The ladies, women, and children, were, during the first day of June, in the main building of the Residency, very closely packed, and many who were fugitives from out-stations in great discomfort.

At this time Company's paper was selling in the city at seventy per cent. discount; and but that officers were only allowed a proportion of their salary equal to subsistence allowance, as the treasure might be required for the future, much money could have been made: it was a wise precaution of Sir Henry; the money might be wanted eventually, and it was all we could ever expect to have.

On the 12th of June, a military police regiment, under the command of Captain A. Orr, mutinied about noon, without showing any previous signs of discontent, and marched out with their arms and accoutrements. A force of about 100 European

Infantry and two horse-artillery guns, with a troop of Sikh horse, pursued, and overtook them some five miles out of the city. The regiment, 700 strong, had made steadily away through the Dilkoosha Park, all scattered over the country; and the cavalry and guns—the infantry not being able to keep up—did not kill more than twenty of them. As the infantry retreated, they kept up a desultory fire on the small party of their assailants, and eventually joined other mutineers at the gathering near Nawabgunge on the Fyzabad road.

This was an unpleasant episode, showing how completely all had determined apparently to throw off British supremacy. Towards the latter end of June, the British forces were collected in the Muchee Bhawun and the Residency; and some native troops were still stationed in the city at a place called the Dowlutkhana.

The late Captain Fulton, of the Engineers, constructed a telegraph on the top of the Residency to correspond with a similar one put up on the fort of the Muchee Bhawun. Patrols were daily sent out in the direction of Nawabgunge, on the Fyzabad road, to bring intimation of the enemy, who showed decided signs of assembling there in force.

It will be well to note here, that the siege of

Cawnpore, at this time going on, was felt with the greatest sympathy by all in Lucknow, and numerous were the projects and designs for crossing the Ganges and aiding the gallant band there besieged. With great interest and patience did the late Sir Henry Lawrence listen to all these proposals; but, comparing the intelligence received from Cawnpore with the plans proposed, and our means for executing them, Sir Henry, with firmness, yet with sorrow, decided he could only do his utmost to save all here—for Cawnpore he could send no aid. At last the news reached us through a letter written by a young officer at Cawnpore to his father at Lucknow, that General Wheeler had agreed to treat with the Nana. Sir Henry at once felt all was over with them, and a few hours brought the sorrowful news. It was no slight addition to his cares to have the painful duty of refusing aid to General Wheeler, whose letters were naturally urgent, and plainly expressed that otherwise all would perish. But the attempt was out of the question. 200 Europeans was the utmost we could have spared, and with this little army, a broad river was to be forced in the teeth of a large force, with a numerous artillery in position, and which, firing from a high bank, fully commanded the passage: even after the crossing had been effected, at least one mile of ground must be passed over before the entrenchment could be reached.

It was with the greatest difficulty any news at all reached us from Cawnpore; all the boats from ten miles up and ten miles down the river, the Nana had carefully collected on his side of the river, and his sowars patrolled the banks for fifteen miles up and down.

About the 20th of June, Captain Gall volunteered to carry despatches for Sir Henry Lawrence to Allahabad. He was an officer of the Madras Army, and commanding an irregular cavalry corps. It was not Sir Henry's wish he should go, but Captain Gall was very confident in the fidelity of his men. When mounted on his horse in his disguise, he told me that he felt certain we should need aid, our position would be much worse than his, he would return from Allahabad, guiding troops to our succour. I pressed his hand as he rode off, and wished him all success, but felt great doubts for his safety. Selecting some six of his men, on whom he believed he could depend, he started and reached Roy Bareilly safely.

There the townsmen got information, by some means or other, that a sahib was in the serai, and a mob collecting, the unfortunate officer was set upon and killed. It appears that the murder was perpetrated by the Mahomedans of the town, and it is not known how far his own sowars were implicated. This expedition of Captain Gall's was undertaken at his own request and against the advice of his friends, who could not but look on it as most perilous, considering the state of Oude, and remembering the fate of poor Captain Hayes and many other Oude officers who had trusted their men.

The health of Sir Henry during these later days was very broken; at times he was so exhausted that it became necessary to appoint a provisional council, who carried on the executive during those days when the doctors absolutely forbade his doing anything.

Mr. Gubbins, financial commissioner; Mr. Ommaney, judicial commissioner; Major Banks, commissioner of Lucknow; Colonel Inglis, of Her Majesty's 32nd Regiment; and Major Anderson, chief engineer, composed this provisional council, with Mr. Couper, the secretary.

Some four days before the siege commenced, the jewels of the ex-king were removed from the Kaiser Bagh to prevent their falling into the hands of the enemy, and were stowed away in the Residency.

To effect this, as opposition was anticipated from the African eunuchs and slaves, two horse-artillery guns and a company of Europeans attended the party. No opposition was offered, but the feelings of the people were pretty clearly expressed by their demeanour.

Major Banks and Captain Carnegie were deputed by Sir Henry Lawrence to seize the jewels, and Major Banks requested me to accompany him. The jewels were in large ant-eaten boxes, whose bottoms dropped out when removed. With great trouble we succeeded in filling a number of boxes with an indiscriminate mass of valuables, including jewels of all sorts, valuable swords, dresses, &c. These boxes having no locks, we tied cords round them and sealed the fastenings.

By this precautionary measure of Sir Henry's, the rebels were deprived of some eighty lakhs of jewels, for which they eagerly inquired when they entered the city: this I have since ascertained from inquiries here.

On the evening of the 29th of June, the enemy having reached Chinhut, a village about eight miles from Lucknow, on the Fyzabad road, it was determined to attack them. The result of this engagement has been already published; but the following extract from the report of Brigadier Inglis will be read again with interest:—

The force destined for this service, and which was composed as follows, moved out at 6 A.M., on the morning of the 30th of June:—

Artillery.—4 guns of No. — Horse Light Field Battery.
4 „ of No. 2, Oude Field Battery.
2 „ of No. 3, Oude Field Battery.
An 8-inch howitzer.

Cavalry.—Troops of Volunteer Cavalry.
120 troopers of detachments, belonging to 1st, 2nd, and 3rd regiments of Oude Irregular Cavalry.

Infantry.—300 Her Majesty's 32nd.
150 13th Native Infantry.
60 48th Native Infantry.
20 71st Native Infantry (Sikhs).

The troops, misled by the reports of wayfarers, who stated that there were few or no men between Lucknow and Chinhut, proceeded somewhat farther than had been originally intended, and suddenly fell in with the enemy, who had, up to that time, eluded the vigilance of the advance guard by concealing themselves behind a long line of trees in overwhelming numbers. The European force and the howitzer, with the Native Infantry, held the foe in check for some time; and had the six guns of the Oude Artillery been faithful, and the Sikh cavalry shown a better front, the day would have been won in spite of an immense disparity in numbers. But the Oude artillerymen and drivers were traitors. They overturned the guns into ditches, cut the traces of their horses, and abandoned them, regardless of the remonstrances and exertions of their own officers and of those of Sir Henry Lawrence's staff, headed by the Brigadier-General in person, who himself drew his sword upon these rebels. Every effort to induce them to stand having proved ineffectual, the force, exposed to a vastly superior fire of artillery, and completely outflanked on both sides by an overpowering body of infantry and cavalry, which actually got into our rear, was compelled to retire with the loss of three pieces of artillery, which fell into the hands of the enemy, in consequence of the rank treachery of the Oude gunners, and with a very grievous list of killed and wounded. The heat was dreadful, the gun ammunition was expended, and the almost total want of cavalry to protect our rear made our retreat most disastrous.

All the officers behaved well; and the exertions of the small body of volunteer cavalry, only forty in number, under Captain Radcliffe, 7th Light Cavalry, were most praiseworthy. Sir Henry Lawrence subsequently conveyed his thanks to myself, who had, at his request, accompanied him upon this occasion (Colonel Case being in command of Her Majesty's 32nd). He also expressed his approbation of the way in which his staff—Captain Wilson, officiating deputy assistant adjutant-general; Lieutenant James, sub-assistant commissary-general; Captain Edgell, officiating military secretary; and Mr. Couper, civil service; the last of whom had acted as Sir Henry Lawrence's aide-de-camp from the commencement of the disturbances—had conducted themselves throughout this arduous day. Sir Henry further particularly mentioned that he would bring the gallant conduct of Captain Radcliffe and of Lieutenant Bonham, of the Artillery (who worked the howitzer successfully until incapacitated by a wound), to the prominent notice of the government of India. The manner in which Lieutenant Birch, 71st Native Infantry, cleared a village with a party of Sikh skirmishers, also elicited the admiration of the Brigadier-General. The conduct of Lieutenant Hardinge, who, with his handful of horse, covered the retreat of the rear-guard, was extolled by Sir Henry, who expressed his intention of mentioning the services of this gallant officer to his lordship in council. Lieutenant-Colonel Case, who commanded Her Majesty's 32nd Regiment, was mortally wounded whilst gallantly leading on his men. The service had not a more deserving officer. The command devolved on Captain Steevens, who also received a death wound shortly afterwards. The command then fell to Captain Mansfield, who has since died of cholera.

Our men reached the Residency utterly exhausted from a terrific sun and a fatiguing retreat; Sir Henry himself returned on a gun carriage. Weak and exhausted by illness before he started, it was a miracle he returned alive. I met him at the door of the Residency as he returned. It needed no words to explain the result; the utterly exhausted state of our poor fellows as they came in told its own tale. An overwhelming force, aided by the defection of our native gunners, brought about the catastrophe.

The enemy pursued, but halted at the iron bridge, which is within the range of the guns both of the Residency and Muchee Bhâwun. They opened a gun on the Residency from the iron bridge, but our fire from the Redan battery soon silenced it. They then gradually spread down on the opposite bank of the river towards the bridge of boats below the palace called the Chuttur Munzil; this Lieutenant Alexander, of the Artillery, soon disabled with an 18-pounder, and they had to move the bridge lower down.

Our working parties had commenced work as usual that day; but, as the firing neared the Residency, an universal flight ensued, and with them a great number of private and public servants.

By evening of that day, the enemy had entirely spread round the entrenchment, though not actually in the very near houses. The richest part of the city, called the "Chouk," was plundered that night by the disorganized rebels, and the citizens began to find out the nature and habits of their invited guests.

The slackness of the investment during this first night and the following were invaluable to the garrison. Many important engineering and other arrangements were effected: Mr. Gubbins succeeded most effectually in entrenching a bastion which I had been making for some days, but was then unfinished; parapets all round were looked to and improved; better arrangements for commissariat stores devised, and many other necessary though minor operations.

On the 1st of July, it was determined to evacuate the Muchee Bhâwun. The order was sent by Captain Fulton's telegraph, and accordingly at 12 P.M., Lieutenant Thomas, of the Artillery, made arrangements for blowing it up when the party marched out.

His arrangements were so perfect and so well executed, that the fort did not blow up until just as the first man reached the Residency, when the whole went off like a huge enormous mine; it was a magnificent spectacle, and no doubt somewhat surprised our assailants, who had permitted the whole Muchee Bhâwun garrison to reach the Residency unmolested.

The following diary by the late Major Banks will be read with great interest; it briefly describes the incidents of the siege up to the day of his death. The original diary, much defaced and blotted, was found in the city by Mr. Kavanagh, assistant commissioner, all written over with native accounts, evidently belonging to some pay havildar of a regiment:—

Lucknow Residency, *2nd July*, 1857.

At a meeting of Major Banks, Colonel Inglis, and Major Anderson, Lucknow, 10.30 A.M., 2nd July, 1857. It has pleased God that Sir Henry Lawrence, K.C.B., Brigadier-General and Chief Commissioner, should be very grievously wounded, it is feared mortally, at 9 A.M., this day. Sir Henry Lawrence had previously notified to government his desire, that, in case of any casualty befalling himself, I (Major Banks) should fulfil the functions of Chief Commissioner, and that Colonel Inglis, her Majesty's 32nd Regiment, commanding all the troops, and Major Anderson, should be a military council.

This morning, after being wounded, and while in the perfect possession of all his faculties, Sir Henry Lawrence publicly delegated the above charge to the respective gentlemen, and these functions have now been provisionally assumed by them.

I announced that Sir Henry Lawrence had just communicated his orders to me personally, in the presence of many gentlemen on the following points:—

I.—Reserve fire, check all wall firing.

II.—Carefully register ammunition for guns and small arms in store. Carefully register daily expenditure as far as possible.

III.—Spare the precious health of Europeans in every possible way, from shot and sun.

IV.—Organize working parties for night labour.

V.—Entrench—entrench—entrench—erect traverses, cut off enemy's fire.

VI.—Turn every horse out of the entrenchment, except enough for four guns. Keep Sir Henry Lawrence's horse "Ludakee;" it is a gift to his nephew, George Lawrence.

VII.—Use the state prisoners as a means of getting in supplies by gentle means if possible, or by threats.

VIII.—Enrol every servant as bildar, or carrier of earth. Pay liberally, double, quadruple.

IX.—Turn out every native who will not work (save menials who have more than abundant labour).

X.—Write daily to Allahabad or Agra.

XI.—Sir Henry Lawrence's servants to receive one year's pay; they are to work for any other gentlemen who want them, or they may leave if they prefer to do so.

XII.—Put on my tomb only this—"Here lies Henry Lawrence, who tried to do his duty. May God have mercy on him."

XIII.—Take an immediate inventory of all natives, so as to know who can be used as bildars, &c.

XIV.—Take an immediate inventory of all supplies and food, &c. Take daily average of expenditure.

The foregoing to be acted on.

It was resolved that Colonel Inglis should receive the local rank of brigadier subject to confirmation. Lieutenant Birch, 71st Native Infantry, to be aide-de-camp, subject to confirmation.

2nd July.—At a meeting, 2 P.M., Major Banks, Colonel Inglis, Major Anderson, Mr. Gubbins, and Mr. Ommaney, present. Mr. Gubbins, financial commissioner, announced that so long as Sir Henry Lawrence lives, he would not record any objection, but would urge his claims to the chief post, should it please God to take Sir Henry. Ordered that this question be left over. "Sufficient for the day is the evil thereof." (Military orders entered in military books.) Wrote to Havelock and to Agra (*see* Captain Edgell's book for letters); could not be sent.

3rd July.—Collect and again tie up the bullocks which have broken out. Turn out horses, all save enough for six guns for the present. Grave-digging parties required. Attend to conservancy. Issue of rations at night, as fire slackens then; double pay to be issued to all soldiers, workmen, bearers, and, in short, to all natives in the public service who work during the present siege, beginning from 1st of July. A grinding corps to be established of dooley-bearers, to be held in the khansamah's house, commissariat department, to make arrangements, more especially as to any special remuneration. (My orders entered in Order-book.) Servants of state prisoners to be allowed to go out to fetch medicines for their masters. Wrote to General Havelock, Allahabad, and to Agra (*see* Captain Edgell's books). Mr. Ommaney, judicial commissioner, grievously wounded by a round shot in the head.

Saturday, 4th July.—Our most honoured chief, Sir Henry Lawrence, K.C.B., has gone to his rest; therefore, under his last orders, delivered before many gentlemen while he was in the full possession of his faculties, Major Banks, Brigadier Inglis, and Major Anderson, assume substantively the functions which they have since the 2nd instant received provisionally. It is generally known, and Mr. Couper, secretary to the Chief Commissioner, can establish the fact, that some time before his death, Sir Henry Lawrence had represented to government that, in his opinion, the public safety would be best consulted by routine being set aside, and by Major Banks being appointed to act as Chief Commissioner (provisionally), assisted by Colonel Inglis and Major Anderson.

Issued orders on the following subjects (*see* my Order-books):—

Commissariat officers to send in immediately lists of stores of all sorts, stating how long the stock of each article is expected to last.

Commissariat officers to send in returns of estimated daily expenditure.

Ordnance commissariat officers to send in returns of estimated daily expenditure.

Commanding officers of corps, regular or irregular, to forward weekly, from to-morrow, statements showing the number of all ranks present, fit for duty, killed, wounded, sick, &c.

Dowlut Sing, private of Lieutenant Bryce's battery, is promoted to havildar, for highly gallant and intrepid service in his battery under heavy fire. To date from the 3rd instant.

Heera Sing, jemadar of the same battery, to be subadar from the 3rd instant, in reward for fidelity and good service.

Officers are requested to bear in mind that they must not, on any account, leave their posts on the occurrence of accident or casualty in another direction. At the fire, last night, several officers from the outposts were seen about, while they should have been at their specific duties, and keeping their men watchful and quiet.

The commissariat officers are called on to exercise strict vigilance over the public stores. The carelessness of a day may be death to us.

It has already been notified that the command is in the hands of Brigadier Inglis. To that officer will be addressed all requests for orders connected with the troops, save only such as refer to the engineering and artillery branches; matters connected with these will be referred to Major

Anderson, engineer, who will pass orders or refer to the senior artillery officer.

For public convenience, the residence of the following officers is notified :—

Major Banks at Mr. Gubbins' house.

Brigadier Inglis, Residency; corner room on ground floor under what was Sir Henry Lawrence's room.

Major Anderson, post-office.

The posts of the several artillery officers will be noted by Brigadier Inglis.

N.B.—Received letters Nos. 1 and 2 from Mr. Gubbins (these and the replies of this date are with Captain Edgell).

Wrote two letters to General Havelock at Allahabad, one by Naeb Kotwal's messenger, who will get 300 rupees if he brings a reply, one by Hawes, and one to Agra *viâ* Mynpoorie, by Hawes.

Sir Henry Lawrence's remains interred at 9.45 P.M., in church inclosure.

Sunday, 5th July, 1857.—Council met at noon. Gave orders regarding conservancy.

Commissariat arrangements.

At 4.30 P.M., Brigadier Inglis and Major Banks, with Major Anderson, decided that a 24-pounder howitzer should not be put on the roof of the Brigade mess-house.

Rain at intervals; enemy's fire on the whole not so heavy.

Cawnpore road battery terribly exposed. No messenger could be got to take letters to Allahabad and Mynpoorie. Thirteen Sikhs deserted during the night. Rumours of further intention of deserting on the part of Sikhs.

Firing heard about four miles (as well as could be guessed) to the south. The flashes seen about sunset; no clue to the cause or circumstances as yet known.

Monday, 6th July.—Firing strangely diminished on the enemy's part. Has this any connection with the native reports that many of the enemy have gone to oppose succours coming to us? Time hardly admits this.

I observed a palisading and new earthwork of the enemy's in the Tehree Kothee compound, also new earthwork opposite Cawnpore road battery.

More defections among the Sikhs reported to be intended.

Carcases poisoning air; get them removed at all hazards.

For letter to Mr. Court, magistrate of Allahabad (*see* Captain Edgell's book), sent by Benee Sookul, invalid, who receives five rupees, and 100 if he brings a reply.

No messenger for Mynpoorie.

Tuesday, 7th July.—Firing of enemy slackened somewhat; very few guns fired by them. At 1.30 P.M., with 1st and Grenadier Company, Her Majesty's 32nd Regiment, and a party of Sikhs, made a dash at Johannes' house, from near which trenches were being cut to the Cawnpore battery, and from which house a galling fire was kept up by the enemy on the battery. Twenty-two of the enemy killed; four of our men wounded only, one badly (Cooney, a gallant fellow, who had spiked a gun of the enemy a few days before). Party most dashingly led by Lieutenant Lawrence, 32nd Regiment, and Ensign Studdy; the whole under Mansfield. It was found that no mining under the "King's Hospital" (in which are many ladies and children) had been attempted by the enemy.

It seems to me to be regretted that the house was not, in some way, rendered untenable as a post on the side towards our defences, for on our quitting it the enemy occupied it again, and fired down the post-office lane at our men passing.

Major Francis shot through both legs by a round shot.

Heavy rain in evening and night.

Received a long letter, No. 3, from Mr. Gubbins, claiming chief civil power.

Wednesday, 8th July.—Rain in morning. Mr. Ommaney died. Mr. Polehampton wounded.

Wrote to Allahabad to Mr. Court (*see* Captain Edgell's book). Enemy's fire slack till evening, when it blazed up about 5.30 P.M.

Sent letter by Soonath Misser, 69th Native Infantry, Naik, 18-pounder battery, down the enemy's cover in the Terhee Kothee.

Much alarm and firing during the night; no real attack attempted.

Major Francis died of his wounds.

Thursday, 9th July.—Rain during the early morning; heavy firing on the part of the enemy. Replied to Mr. Gubbins' letter No. 3 (*see* Mr. Couper's letter book).

Men sent out: tell us that, save at Golagunge and Fuckeer Mahomed's house, there are not many mutinous soldiers. There is a party at Mr. Hill's shops, about sixty; also three hundred in the old Cotwally building. Many said to have gone to their homes in disgust. Some regiments said to have gone against the force advancing from Allahabad. This is denied by others.

Very few large guns fired at us for the last three days.

13th Mutineers Native Infantry 48th Mutineers Native Infantry 4th Oude Irregular Force Infantry 7th Oude Irregular Force Infantry 5th Oude Irregular Force Infantry	Said to be investing us, but I think this can hardly be right.

Friday, 10th July.—A native emissary stated that Cawnpore

is occupied by the English. I therefore wrote a letter thither, sending it by Bhoopchund Naik, invalid, at 9.15 P.M.

I also wrote to Mr. Court, at Allahabad, and sent it by Bhowany Deen Tewarry, havildar of invalids, at 9.15 P.M. I could not get a messenger for Mynpoorie.

Mr. Elliott, a writer, disguised himself and brought in news from the town, but of a preposterous nature, dealing in tens of thousands, and evidently wrong. He says, however, that four regiments, with six guns, had been sent by the Nana Sahib from Cawnpore to intercept relief to us, and that an attack was to be made at 4 A.M. to-morrow, the forlorn hope being five hundred Passees, to whom great promises have been made. Warned all guards.

Saturday, 11*th July*.—No attack last night.

Addressed Brigadier Inglis regarding the treasure and the copper caps said to have been brought from the Muchee Bhâwun by the troops under Colonel Palmer, and of which treasure and caps no information can, I am told, be now got here.

Addressed Brigadier Inglis regarding the bringing of the valuables belonging to the king brought from the Kaiser Bagh.

Addressed Brigadier Inglis and Major Anderson regarding the remarks made by Mr. Ommaney at our meeting of the 2nd instant, on the subject of the arrangements ordered by Sir Henry Lawrence, for the conduct of affairs.

No messenger could be procured for Allahabad.

Sunday, 12*th July*.—Enemy not very active during the day. They, however, took possession (yesterday) of a house about one hundred yards from Mr. Gubbins' post, from which they annoyed us a good deal. The commanding officer of Mr. Gubbins' post had fired some 9-pounder round shot at the house; but Brigadier Inglis forbade this, for obvious reasons. He caused some shells to be thrown, which turned the enemy out.

At night, an attack on the river-side of the Residency repulsed and some fifty of the enemy killed; no loss on our side.

No messenger procurable to send letters out.

Because of gram instead of flour being used, several khidmutgars and bheestees bolted. Mr. G. had agreed to arrange for grinding, but each servant had to grind his own, and these hard-worked fellows could not stand this.

Monday, 13*th July*.—Enemy fired back upon us three shells of our own (eight-inch) which had not exploded, and to which they fitted new fuses. They also fired a carcass as a round shot. It traversed the mess room in the Residency, but fortunately struck no one.

Lieutenant Charlton struck in the head by a bullet; very dangerous wound.

No very great activity on the part of the enemy.

At night I was well enough to visit some of the posts. All well.

Night wet; earthwork protection thrown up to protect entrance to post-office.

Tuesday, 14*th July*.—Morning cloudy.

Enemy very active, firing heavily with musketry, and they have moved more guns close to Mr. Gubbins near the yellow house, and also a gun to the back of the King's Hospital. This has done some harm, putting six round shot in half an hour through the wall, and carrying off an Englishman's legs.

Lieutenant Lester severely (mortally, it is feared) hit through the back by a musket bullet, which came sweeping over from the Redan side.

Wrote to Cawnpore and Allahabad (or force on march); letter sent by Goolab, who is to receive two hundred rupees for an answer.

Fine night; not much firing.

Wednesday, 15*th July*.—Much firing in the morning; subsided towards noon. Fine day. The stench of dead horses buried outside the intrenchment very unpleasant.

Wrote to Cawnpore and Allahabad; sent letters by a jemadar, 71st Native Infantry.

Firing blazed up in the evening.

Thursday, 16*th July*.—Nothing of special note. Enemy less troublesome than usual. No rain.

No messenger procurable to carry letters to the outside.

Lester died. Mrs. Thomas died of confluent small-pox in the Begum's Kothee.

Firing blazed up at night a good deal. Fine night.

Bryce shot through thigh by musket-ball.

Friday, 17*th July*.—Nothing of special note. Heavy firing at night, but little injury done.

No messenger procurable.

Clare Alexander, Artillery, terribly burnt by a mortar.

Saturday, 18*th July*.—Heavy firing in the morning; firing mitigated during the afternoon.

Letter to Cawnpore sent by Mr. Alexander, a writer.

Letter to Allahabad or advancing force, sent by Isseree Gwalla.

Much firing during the night.

Sunday, 19*th July*.—Lieutenant Arthur killed in Cawnpore battery. Lieutenant Harmer lost leg from round shot.

Seven round shot through drawing-room of Mr. Gubbins' house.

The lamented Major Banks, whose journal here terminates, was killed on the 21st July, shot through the head by a bullet: he died at once.

At the time of his death he was on the roof of a stable in Mr. Gubbins' compound, on the side where the enemy was making a very determined attack.

As a member of the garrison, I may state how deeply all felt his loss. I know that he had previously enjoyed the entire confidence of the late lamented Sir Henry Lawrence, K.C.B., to whom he was a most valuable and ever ready counsellor. Capable of undergoing incessant fatigue, both of mind and body, he gave confidence to all, as much by his bodily presence where danger was most imminent, as by his sound, firm, and judicious orders.

I trust it may be admissible here to allude, but briefly, to the services I myself saw rendered by the civilians, covenanted and uncovenanted. An eye-witness, I saw Mr. Gubbins, the financial commissioner, labouring incessantly either at the defensive works of his own garrison, or defending with his rifle some weak part. To him is due the credit of having retrenched and completed his bastion. On the very first night of the siege he proposed it to me, and, by his energy and perseverance, effectually carried it out.

I saw Mr. Couper, the secretary to the Chief Commissioner, aided by three or four other civilians between the intervals of "sentry go," labouring with spade and shovel in heat and in rain, in the revolting task of burying the putrid carcases of bullocks; and I have felt most grateful for his example and strong right arm in labouring at the shafts and mines of the Brigade mess. The friend and counsellor of Sir John Inglis, K.C.B., he was ever as ready to aid him manually as mentally. Night after night I have seen him with Major Wilson, our vigilant and valued adjutant-general, going round to all the garrisons of our position, to be able to report to Sir John that the utmost watchfulness prevailed in all.

I witnessed Mr. Martin the deputy commissioner's exertions before the siege, in procuring that to which, under Providence, we owe our lives, namely, provisions; and I saw how he always lent a hand to any work going on in addition to his own daily sentry duty.

The gallantry and devoted bravery of Mr. Thornhill is known to all. I had personally observed it when he joined in the pursuit of a mutinous Oude police regiment before the siege commenced; and I saw him on his deathbed, where he sealed his devotion with his life. As a voluntary guide to bring in the wounded of the late Sir Henry Havelock's force, he had gone out from the garrison, and in that noble duty received his death wound.

The vigilance and cheerfulness of Mr. Schilling, principal of La Martinière College, and Mr. Shank, professor in the same, both of whom, aided by some soldiers, managed by their schoolboys to guard most effectually their important post, was well known to all: and in our mining operations at their post I could not but observe their cordial ever ready aid.

In the labours of the mines at Sago's and the Financial garrisons, the constant hard work of the uncovenanted of those excellent garrisons was most conspicuous. It is not possible to mention all, but the few facts I have mentioned will prove how nobly the Civil Service, covenanted and uncovenanted, took up its allotted part in the defence of the garrison, rendering, by its hearty union, that garrison within able effectually to repel the unwieldy and providentially disunited efforts of the vast hordes without.

The remaining particulars of the siege of Lucknow and its splendid relief, under the late General Sir Henry Havelock, K.C.B., with General Sir

James Outram, G.C.B., who so nobly seconded him, have become history; it remains only to trace out the fate of those of our surviving countrymen and women who, unable to reach the Residency before the siege commenced, could not afterwards come in.

It will be remembered that a small party escaped from Setapore and joined Captain Patrick Orr and his wife at Mithowlee.

This party consisted of Sir Mountstewart Jackson, Bart., and his sister, Miss Jackson; Lieutenant Burnes, 10th Oude Irregular Infantry; Sergeant-Major Morton; and Miss Sophie Christian, a little child only three years old.

It will also be remembered that the Shahjehanpore fugitives were stated to have been massacred in the northern part of Oude.

A complete account of the Shahjehanpore massacre and the fortunes of Captain Orr and his wife and child, and of Sir M. Jackson's party, is given as follows, by Captain Alexander Orr, a deputy commissioner in Oude.*

* Note by Captain Hutchinson:—"I may observe here that on the 10th May I was with Mr. Thomason and Captain Orr at Mohumdee, and that on the 13th May I left Captain James's house at Shahjehanpore, at which time the utmost peace and security apparently reigned at both places."

On the 31st of May, 1857, Sunday, the mutiny broke out at Shahjehanpore. Most of the officers and ladies of the station were assembled at church. The building was suddenly surrounded by rebel sepoys, who, rushing in, murdered many of the congregation; some, however, of the officers and ladies succeeded in obtaining refuge in the vestry and turret of the church, securing the door after them. Fortunately, the sepoys were only armed with swords and latthees, and their efforts to break open the doors being unsuccessful, they withdrew to their lines for the purpose of arming themselves with their muskets, with which to renew the attack. Seizing upon the opportunity of escape thus afforded to them, the officers and ladies rushed to some carriages and horses still waiting outside of the building; and, mounting, made the best of their way to Powaen, the residence of a rajah, and situated on the frontier of Oude, but within the Shahjehanpore district. The party was ill received by the rajah, who, urging his inability, real or pretended, to protect them, refused them shelter. Mr. Jenkins, the junior magistrate of Shahjehanpore, and one of the party, on his arrival at Powaen, wrote to Mr. Thomason, the deputy commissioner of Mohumdee, in Oude, giving him notice of what had occurred at Shahjehanpore, and begging him to send all available carriage to enable the party to reach Mohumdee. Mr. Thomason received the letter at the hands of a runner on the evening of the 31st of May, and immediately complied with Mr. Jenkins' request.

Previous to this period, matters had been wearing a gloomy aspect at Mohumdee. It is true that, up to the 3rd of June, 1857, the daks were still running, but it had also become evident that the minds of the native population were greatly agitated. At the station were Mr. Thomason, the deputy commissioner, and Captain Patrick Orr, first assistant commissioner, with Mrs. Orr and child. Of troops there were, two companies of the 9th Regiment Oude Irregular Force, two companies of the Oude Military Police, with about fifty troopers.

On the receipt of Mr. Jenkins' letter, both Mr. Thomason and Captain Orr felt that the crisis was at hand, and that the mutineers of the 28th Regiment Native Infantry, from Shahjehanpore, would shortly reach Mohumdee, attracted thither by the hope of securing for themselves the contents of the Government treasury. It was at once resolved that Mrs. Orr should be sent to Mithowlee, under care of the rajah of that place,—a man who had not only been ever treated with much consideration by Mr. Thomason, but also was indebted to Captain Orr for many acts of kindness shown to him by that officer, before the country had passed under British rule. It was also resolved that the civil officers should withdraw from the station to the fort of Mohumdee, distant about one mile. The fort had, since the annexation, been made use of as a treasury as well as a gaol. Mr. Thomason even hoped that he might, in case of necessity, by strengthening the fort and calling for assistance from the neighbouring zemindars, defend the place against the attacks of the rebels; but it was soon found that the building was in too dilapidated a state to admit of its long being taken advantage of as a place of defence.

On the night, then, of the 31st of May, 1857, Mrs. Orr, accompanied by an escort of the 9th Regiment Oude Irregular Infantry, under command of Issuree Sing, subadar, left Mohumdee; the escort having previously sworn to defend with their lives both Mrs. Orr and her child. The small party marched all night, a distance of about twenty-six miles, and reached Mithowlee on the morning of the 1st June, at about eight o'clock. On the arrival at the fort of the rajah, Mrs. Orr was told that he was asleep, and could not, on any account, be disturbed. At the expiration of two long and weary hours the rajah sent his vakeel with a message to Mrs. Orr that she should proceed to another of his forts, at a place called Kutcheanee, situated in a dense jungle, and, consequently, as he said, less likely to attract the attention of the bands of soldiers that it was expected would shortly be overrunning the country.

Finding all remonstrances useless, Mrs. Orr proceeded with her escort to the Kutcheanee fort, on entering which a place was pointed out for herself and another for the escort. It was a most dreary, desolate-looking building, devoid of the most common articles of furniture, and presenting a picture of the utmost discomfort. Mrs. Orr could not but shudder as she entered the place, but she was assured by the people that the rajah would himself shortly come to the fort, and make every arrangement for her comfort. He did, indeed, come that very evening, and, taking a most solemn oath, assured his guest that he would be faithful to her and protect her from all danger. He mentioned, in course of conversation, that Mr. Christian, the commissioner of the division, had written to him to forward to Setapore all the rajah's elephants, but that he had refused to comply with the commissioner's request, under pretext that the animals were suffering from sore backs; but he plainly gave Mrs. Orr to understand that, although Setapore had not as yet broken out, still the men were ripe for mutiny, and he did not wish to lose his elephants.

The rajah, after renewing his protestations of fidelity, took his departure for Mithowlee, without, however, having taken any steps towards rendering her position a little less uncomfortable, or providing for her most pressing wants. The whole day had passed, and the evening was fast closing in, without any food having been supplied, and it was only at a late hour of the night that some provisions of a coarse kind were procured from a village. Those who are unacquainted with the manners and customs of the Oude zemindars, and who have experienced the courteous hospitality invariably shown by them to strangers, will not fail to remark this gross deviation on the part of the rajah from time-honoured usage.

Let us now return to Mohumdee. On the receipt by Mr. Thomason of Mr. Jenkins' letter, he sent for a party of men from the lines to escort to the fort a sum of money which was then in the kutcherry. The men came; but though they still, mechanically as it were, obeyed orders, yet from their behaviour and bearing, it was but too evident that they were no longer under any real subordination. It was also from this party that the escort which accompanied Mrs. Orr to Mithowlee had been chosen. They belonged to the regiment formerly raised and commanded by Captain Orr under the Oude rule. That officer now advanced to the sepoys, and plainly and frankly told them that the troops at Shahjehanpore had mutinied, and that, in all probability, sooner or later, they would come to Mohumdee; that he was anxious to see Mrs. Orr and her child placed in safety; that he had fixed upon Mithowlee as a place of refuge, and that he now asked them, if they would escort them to the rajah's fort. The men swore solemnly to do so.

Issuree Sing, subadar, at once came forward and said that not only would he accompany them to Mithowlee, but even, should it be desired, he would see them safely to Lucknow. To this latter proposal, however, the men objected, saying that Lucknow was at too great a distance, but they would willingly agree to go to Mithowlee. We have seen how well they fulfilled their promise. Issuree Sing, especially, behaved extremely well, showing in his conduct the greatest respect towards Mrs. Orr, and even, when required, affording his assistance and advice. On Mrs. Orr's departure from Mohumdee, Mr. Thomason and Captain Orr, followed by the troops then at Mohumdee, removed to the fort. This was now the 1st of June. On the day following, the party expected from Powaen reached Mohumdee. It must not be imagined that the officers who had escaped from Shahjehanpore had effected their escape scathless; no, several of them had received severe wounds, which had been bound up by the ladies of the party with portions of their dress torn up for the purpose.

Sad was the appearance of the poor Shahjehanpore refugees on their arrival at Mohumdee; weary and with naked feet did they with much difficulty and toil reach thus far. Mr. Thomason now wrote to Mr. Christian, at Setapore, requesting him to send all the conveyances he could possibly collect for the use of the party at Mohumdee, whose intention it was to proceed to Setapore, then considered the safest place. Mr. Christian sent the carriages, together with a guard, which reached Mohumdee on the 3rd, and immediately spread the report that two companies of their own regiment had been destroyed by the English at Lucknow for refusing to become Christians. On the following day, the 4th, the guard broke up the dhoolies, &c., that had been entrusted to them by Mr. Christian. It was on the evening of this very day (4th) that all the party then assembled at Mohumdee commenced their march towards Setapore. An account of this dreadful march is contained in the following copy of a letter, written on the 8th June by Captain Orr to his youngest brother at Lucknow. It will be found of a profoundly sad interest, written as it was so shortly after the enactment of the dreadful tragedy of which it gives the details:—

Jungle, near Mithowlee,
8th June, 1857.

MY DEAR ADOLPHE,

I wrote to you on the 6th instant, but am afraid my letter has not been sent to you. On the 31st May, Sunday, the 28th Native Infantry broke out into mutiny, and some of the men rushed into the church and murdered Collector Ricketts, and wounded Spens of the 28th, and killed the doctor. James was killed on his parade ground.

The following made their escape:—

Captains Sneyd, Lysaght, Salmon; Lieutenants Key, Robertson, Scott, Pitt, Rutherford; Ensigns Spens, Johnston, Scott; Quartermaster-Sergeant Grant, Band-master, one drummer, Mrs. Scott, Miss Scott, Mrs. Lysaght, Mrs. Key, Mrs. Bowling, Mrs. Shiels, Mrs. Grant, Mrs. ——, four children, Lieutenant Shiels (Veteran Establishment), Mr. Jenkins, C.S. They ran away to Powaen; but the rajah turned them out the next morning, and they came to Mohumdee. Thomason, the deputy commissioner of Mulaon, and myself, on hearing of this sad affair at Shahjehanpore, consulted together, and sent away Annie to Mithowlee, and went ourselves to the fort to protect the treasury, if possible.

On Monday, about twelve at noon, the party from Shahjehanpore arrived; and from that time the most alarming symptoms showed themselves amongst the men. I used every measure in my power to pacify them, but in vain. By the most strenuous efforts, I persuaded them from hour to hour to come back to their allegiance. Every moment seemed to be our last. The men were civil to me to the last, but each one said he could not answer for what some of the bad characters would do.

I succeeded in gaining some influence over them, and kept them quiet till a detachment of fifty men came in on Tuesday morning (4th) from Setapore, sent by Christian (commissioner) to escort the ladies in.

These men brought with them the report that the whole of their light company at Muchee Bhawun had been cut up by the Europeans, and that they were determined to take their revenge. Seeing the state of things, I sent for all the native officers, and told them to let me know at once, like men, what their intentions were, and, if reasonable, I would give my consent. They came to the resolution of marching at once to Setapore, and swore they would spare our lives, and take Thomason and me into Setapore, and would allow the others to go away unmolested.

I made them take a solemn oath, and they all put their hands on Lutchmun jemadar. Well, we left Mohumdee at 5.30 P.M., on Thursday, after the men had secured the treasure—about one lakh and ten thousand rupees—and released the prisoners. I put as many of the ladies as I could into the buggy, others on the baggage carts, and we reached Burwan at about 10.30 P.M. Next morning—Friday, the 5th—we marched towards Aurungabad. When we had come about two koss, the halt was sounded, and a trooper told us to go on ahead where we liked. We went on for some distance, when we saw a party coming along. They soon joined us and followed the buggy, which we were pushing on with all our might. When within half a mile of Aurungabad, a sepoy rushed forward and snatched Key's gun from him, and shot down poor old Shiels, who was riding my horse. Then the most infernal carnage ever witnessed by man began. We all collected under a tree close by, and put the ladies down from the buggy. Shots were firing in all directions amidst the most fearful yells. The poor ladies all joined in prayer, coolly and undauntedly awaiting their fate. I stopped for about three minutes amongst them, but thinking of my poor wife and child here, I endeavoured to save my life for their sakes. I rushed out towards the insurgents; and one of our men—Goordeen, 6th Company—called out to me to throw down my pistol, and he would save me. I did so, when he put himself between me and the men, and several others followed his example. In about ten minutes more they completed their hellish work. I was about three hundred yards at the utmost. Poor Lysaght was kneeling out in the open ground, with his hands folded across his chest; and though not using his firearms, the cowardly wretches would not go up to him till they shot him, and then, rushing forward, they killed the wounded and the children, butchering them in the most cruel way. With the exception of the drummer boy, every one was killed of the above list, and, besides, poor good Thomason and our two clerks, the bodies being denuded of their clothes for the sake of plunder. They had on them one thousand rupees; and Thomason, one hundred rupees. We had managed to get this money, and distributed it amongst ourselves in case of our escaping. On arrival at Aurungabad, some of the men proposed that I should send for Annie, and, marching into Setapore, put myself at the head of the regiment.

To this, I said I could do nothing without knowing what

the officers said. Fortunately, these were not brutally inclined just then, and explained to the men that it was only by the consent of these two companies that I had escaped, and that there was no knowing what the rest of the corps and the 41st and 10th would say or do, and that till their wish was known, it was better for me to go to Mithowlee. They let me have a horse and a few clothes (they had the evening before plundered Thomason's and my property). I persuaded a guard to bring me here, and got a letter from them, making me over to the Rajah Lonee Sing. On reaching this, the rajah received me, and sent me to the house a koss off, where Annie had been. We remained all Saturday there; and, Sunday morning, the rajah's people, hearing of the mutineers coming to Mithowlee, advised us to remove into the jungle. Here we are since yesterday morning exposed to the most trying heat without any shelter from the sun, except a few thin branches and a sheet we have put up. Moonshee Seetaram is with us, sharing our trouble. I was obliged to part with Bolakee and his party when we were coming here. A few of our faithful servants are hovering about. Our khidmutgars walked off with our forks and pots. Some of the rajah's people feed us; but you may fancy what our appetites are. My poor wife, as usual, is bearing up with her misfortune like a saint, but is extremely weak. The rajah sends word that he will do his best to protect us. The troops from Mohumdee and Setapore are continually moving backwards and forwards between Setapore and Aurungabad; we cannot find out their intentions. Perhaps they will go to Delhi. Some talk of going there, some to Lucknow. They cannot, I hear, decide about the distribution of the money, and there might be a row. My opinion is, that they will all by degrees walk home. You must have heard of the massacre of Setapore: three men, one lady, and one child are here also, but separate from us. The rajah thinks it advisable to divide us, so as to have smaller parties. He is right. From what I can gather, I think that young Jackson, his sister, little Sophia Christian, and Barnes are in the number: I cannot make out the third name. The rajah sent me word, that when the mutineers leave the vicinity, he would try and send me to Lucknow. Show this to Sir H. Lawrence. Tell him that my being here is kept a profound secret. If in a few days something favourable turns up, we might be saved; but I fear nature will not stand much longer. I use my influence in behalf of the other fugitives in having food, &c., sent to them. They are in a house, but do not know where I am. For the safety of both parties, I have not attempted to see them.

My dearest brother, I wrote you a long letter from Mohumdee on the 2nd or 3rd; but as the carnage at Setapore took place on that day, I do not think my letter could have reached you. In that I asked you to do your best, in case of our succumbing to the dreadful privations we are subjected to (even water being with difficulty procurable), for our poor Pauline and Douglas.

I heard to-day that two Europeans had escaped to Dile, and that John Hearsey had gone away somewhere on his elephant. Are any European regiments coming to Lucknow? One regiment sent out towards Setapore would settle this part of the province.

9th.—I could not send this off this morning. I managed to communicate with the other poor fugitives by letter to-day. Seetaram carried the letter. Their names are Sir M. Jackson and sister, little Sophia Christian, Barnes, and Quartermaster Sergeant, 10th Oude Irregulars. I have a servant to cook for us, and he feeds the poor people. The troops are still at Maholee. They cannot make up their minds as to their movements. This morning they went some distance toward Aurung-

13

abad with the intention of going to Delhi, but changed their minds again and returned to Maholee, *en route* to Lucknow. They are constantly quarrelling about the division of their booty; a small body of Europeans could snatch the money from them very easily. The men from Setapore have two lakhs, the Mohumdee detachment 1,10,000. The natives all seem to think that Muchee Bhawun is impregnable. The privations we are put to are indescribable, but the fearful heat beats all; we could put up with anything else. Annie is as well as can be expected. Poor Louisa is behaving like a sensible person, never once troubling for anything. I keep this open to the last in hopes of hearing from the mutineers' camp.

10.5 P.M.—The Passee came back last evening with the news that all the mutineers are collected at Maholee, but cannot make up their minds, they are quarrelling about the money. Some sepoys have as much as eight or nine hundred rupees each; such fellows will walk home.

(Signed) P. J. ORR.

It will be as well to mention, that during the night previous to the massacre, the native officer, Lutchmun, whose name is mentioned in Captain Orr's letter, came to him privately, and, with tears in his eyes, supplicated him to leave the party and proceed to join his wife at Mithowlee, adding that the men had consented to allow him to leave the camp. Captain Orr replied that he could not abandon his friends at a time of such extreme danger, and that unless the whole party were allowed to go unmolested, his fate should be linked with theirs. Lutchmun, notwithstanding Captain Orr's reiterated questions, refused to be more explicit, throwing out merely dark hints as to the fate of the party, but urging and imploring Captain Orr to leave the camp. Lutchmun only left when he found his entreaties of no avail.

The kindly interest shown by Lutchmun, and subsequently by other men of his corps, towards Captain Orr, will be easily explained by a reference to a remark already made, that these men belonged to a corps raised and commanded by Captain Orr previous to annexation.

To render the letter that we have just transcribed more complete, it is merely necessary to add, that when the men, who had escorted Captain Orr to Mithowlee, reached their destination, they bound the rajah down under the most solemn oaths to protect Captain Orr, his wife, and child. To the list given in the letter of those that fell in the massacre at Aurungabad must be added the names of Mr. Thomason and of his two writers, Mr. Smith and his wife, and Mr. Hurst. Mr. Hurst had brought a small Bible with him, the pages of which were eagerly read by the doomed party on their way from Mohumdee towards Setapore. After the massacre the precious volume was picked up by the sole survivor and carefully carried away.

The narrative now returns to the position of Mrs. Orr and her husband, which Captain Orr thus resumes. On that day (the 6th) the rajah sent word to Captain Orr that the number of Europeans under his protection had now become too considerable to admit of their being together at Kutcheanee, and that for safety sake he wished to locate them separately; consequently it was his desire that Captain and Mrs. Orr should leave the fort of Kutcheanee and betake themselves to the jungles (which abound at Mithowlee), and that the new arrivals should occupy Kutcheanee. Why the rajah thus wished to drive Captain Orr and his wife into the jungles, to make room for the new party, and why he did not rather choose for the latter the newly devised place of concealment is still a matter of mystery. However, on the morning of the 7th June, Captain Orr and his wife and child left the fort and proceeded about two miles to the jungle. By this term the reader must not understand a beautiful or even an ordinary *forest*, the noble trees of which would have afforded a grateful and necessary shade, but he must picture to himself a vast and dreary extent of land, covered, with the exception of a few patches here and there, with thorny brushwood, growing to the height of about two or three feet, totally incapable of affording shelter against the fierce and intolerable rays of the scorching sun of India, during this season of the year. What their sufferings were in this wilderness is touchingly described by Captain Orr himself in the letter already given.

As night closed in our poor sufferers were obliged to leave the thickly studded portions of the jungle and remove to an open spot, in order, by lighting fires, &c. to scare away the tigers, wolves, and other wild animals, which infested the neighbourhood. The zemindar of Kutcheanee, one Bustee Sing, sent food, dal, and chuppatees, to the party. This food, of the coarsest description, was served on broad leaves tacked together with thorns.

Captain Orr discovered with great difficulty that the fugitives that had arrived at Mithowlee from Setapore were—1st, Sir Mountstewart Jackson; 2nd, his sister, Miss Madeline Jackson; 3rd, Lieutenant Barnes, who had been doing duty with the 10th Regiment Oude Irregular Force; 4th, Sergeant-Major Morton, of the same corps; and 5th, Miss Sophia Christian, a little child of about three years of age. Since their removal from Mithowlee to the fort of Kutcheanee (after Captain Orr's departure from the latter place), Lonee Sing had completely neglected them; but, as will be seen from his letter, Captain Orr did his utmost to provide for their wants.

A few words will explain how Sir M. Jackson's party reached Mithowlee.

When the massacre at Setapore took place, Sir Mountstewart Jackson, with his sister, Miss M. Jackson, effected his escape and fled from the cantonment, wandering he knew not whither. In the same manner did Lieutenant Barnes, with Sergeant-Major Morton, escape, snatching up in their flight poor little Sophia Christian. After wandering, every moment in danger of their lives, through, to them, an unknown country, they were directed by some village people to Mithowlee as being the only place in the neighbourhood capable of affording them refuge. After enduring many hardships, the wanderers met in a village, a short distance from Mithowlee, and proceeded in company to seek protection from the rajah.

On their arrival, they were refused admittance into the fort, but Lieutenant Barnes, determined at all hazards to obtain an interview with Lonee Sing, boldly rushed through the wicket of the grand doorway, and thus forced an entrance; but in doing so, he was struck on the head by one of the retainers of the rajah and severely wounded. Lonee Sing, seeing him covered with blood, ordered him and his companions to be received into the fort. They were located in a common cowshed. It will be easy to imagine in what a sad plight Lonee Sing's guests were ; completely worn out, as they were, by fatigue, their clothes or rather the little of them that still hung upon them in tatters, without any shoes, and their feet lacerated by the thorns of the jungle through which they had passed.

They arrived at Mithowlee on the morning of the 5th. In the night of the day following they were sent to Kutcheanee.

In the meantime the troops from Shahjehanpore, Mohumdee, and Setapore were continually hovering about the neighbourhood, evidently uncertain what steps to take, whether to proceed to Lucknow and swell the rebel army there, or to march to Delhi. They at last assembled at Maholee, a place situated about fourteen miles from Mithowlee; but their presence in the vicinity caused our people much anxiety and discomfort, and obliged them constantly to change their place of concealment. At last, on the 18th of June, the troops were invited by Rajah Newab Alee to proceed to his place at Mahomdabad, about twenty-eight or thirty miles north-east of Lucknow. This rajah was the first of his class in Oude to raise the standard of revolt, and has since shown himself the bitter enemy of the British. On the departure of the rebels from Maholee, Lonee Sing sent word to Captain Orr, that he might now return to Kutcheanee.

This message was gladly received, as, by returning to the fort, shelter from the sun would at last be obtained. Situated, as our people were, far from all aid, with no Europeans nearer than at Lucknow, and the whole country unfriendly, it will be readily supposed that communication with Lucknow was most difficult and uncertain; however, one faithful servant, by name Purwannee, never for a moment thought of abandoning his master, Captain Orr, and by his means a letter was despatched to that officer's youngest brother and to Sir Henry Lawrence, the then Chief Commissioner of Oude.

Purwannee succeeded in reaching the capital, and brought back with him answers to Captain Orr's letters, as also a purwannah addressed by Sir Henry Lawrence to Lonee Sing, ordering this latter to escort the whole party to Lucknow, and promising him handsome rewards on his arrival. Previous to this, the same request had already over and over again been made by Captain Orr to the rajah, who invariably replied that he should comply with it, and that to enable him to do so, he was collecting his men from the neighbouring villages, and the same answer did he give on perusal of Sir Henry Lawrence's purwannah. It was evident that it was not his desire to get rid of the fugitives. He verily believed that the English rule was at an end, and that he might subsequently make better use of the Europeans now in his custody, than by making them over to the British authorities at Lucknow.

On the 30th of June, 1857, after the disastrous affair at Chinhut, the siege of Lucknow had commenced. The news of the victory the rebels had obtained at Chinhut spread far and wide into the district. Anarchy and confusion commenced; the boy Birjees Kudr, the supposed son of the ex-king Wajid Alee Shah, was placed on the throne, and a royal salute, in honour of the event, was fired at Mithowlee, on the 5th, by Rajah Lonee Sing. Despair filled the hearts of our poor people as they heard the cannon sound from the ramparts of the fort of Mithowlee—despair which increased on the receipt of a message sent to them by the rajah, that they had better leave his place, as he could no longer protect them. Cruel mockery on his part!—whither could they go, surrounded as they were by danger on every side, and with no prospect of meeting with a friendly refuge to cheer them on, and induce them to take a hazardous journey? The very Passees, dependants of the rajah, set to protect, or perhaps rather to guard, the inmates of Kutcheanee, told them candidly on no account to leave their present place of refuge, as most probably, the moment they were out of his estate, he would behave treacherously towards them. In what agony of mind were they plunged!—helpless and without hope! The day passed in solemn silence, no one daring to offer consolation or hope, when none existed in the heart of any. Depart they, therefore, could not, but remained in their wretched place of confinement, each day passing on without affording a single ray of hope that their fortunes would mend. The rajah continued to feed his prisoners (for such they must now be called), but allowing only four pounds of flour and a small pittance of ghee for the whole party. Fortunately, in her flight from Mohumdee, Mrs. Orr had contrived to carry a little money with her, and this was now of the greatest assistance, as she was enabled to add to the pittance given daily by the rajah, by purchasing supplies from a neighbouring market held every eighth day.

We will now pass on to the end of July. The intervening period was passed miserably and sadly. It was well known that disasters had occurred at

Chinhut and at Lucknow; but even that fatal news was by the rajah and his people distorted and exaggerated, and they were anxious to lead their captives to believe that the Muchee Bhawun had fallen into the hands of the rebel soldiery, and that the Residency could not be held by the British for any length of time. It is now useless to add that the Muchee Bhawun had been abandoned and partially blown up by Sir Henry Lawrence himself, and that this story had merely been circulated in order to increase the horror of the situation in which our people were already plunged. As to the probability, or rather certainty, of the Residency falling into the hands of the enemy—an event so confidently calculated upon by the rajah—the glorious and successful defence of that post by a handful of Europeans against the combined efforts of myriads of cowardly ruffians has already shown how the hopes of the rajah on that point were destined to be deceived. But the absence of all intercourse with their own countrymen left them in total and cruel ignorance of all that was being enacted in the country, and, with minds already overwrung with agony, they were forced almost, however reluctantly, to give credit to what was so industriously and with such apparent truth related to them.

Besides the person mentioned in this narrative as having been saved from the massacre of Setapore, another party had also been fortunate enough to effect their escape. This party was guided in their wanderings to the fort of the Rajah of Dhowrairah, in Oude, by Captain John Hearsey, who had commanded the 2nd Regiment Oude Military Police, then stationed at Setapore. Several persons composed this party; amongst others, Miss Georgiana Jackson, the sister of Sir Mountstewart Jackson. Towards the latter end of June, Captain Hearsey succeeded in communicating with our people at Kutcheanee, and it was with no little delight that Sir Mountstewart and his sister heard, for the first time, that their sister had also been saved. Alas! her escape was only a temporary one! She, with several other companions, was treacherously betrayed by the Ranee of Dhowrairah, sent to Lucknow, and, on Sir James Outram's advance on Lucknow, in September, 1857, cruelly put to death.

We must now introduce to the notice of the reader a person who was destined to exercise no little evil influence on the fate of those whose suffering forms the subject of these pages—we allude to one Zahoor-ool Hussein. Before the annexation of Oude, a friend at Bareilly had written to Captain Orr, requesting him to exert himself in procuring, in Oude, employment for this person, in whom he took great interest. Zahoor-ool Hussein, bearer of the letter above alluded to, presented himself, with all the appearance of poverty and wretchedness, to Captain Orr, in 1851. He was, of course, treated with great kindness, fed and clothed, and steps were taken to obtain a suitable situation for him. His accomplishments consisted in his being a good Persian scholar. After some unsuccessful efforts in other quarters, Captain Orr at last obtained for him the much-coveted appointment of vakeel of Lonee Sing, Rajah of Mithowlee. We say "coveted," because, being vakeel to a rajah or any influential landholder in Oude, was being entrusted with much power; the rajah seldom acting or taking any important step without consulting his vakeel; indeed, in many cases, the vakeel was, virtually, the master of the estate. Zahoor-ool Hussein, then, could not but consider his fortune made, when, through Captain Orr's influence, so kindly exerted in his favour, he was appointed the vakeel of the Mithowlee raj. He was not long in ingratiating himself in his new master's favour, and, to make use of a native expression, Lonee Sing only "saw through his vakeel's eyes." Poverty was now exchanged for comparative affluence, and, day by day, Zahoor-ool Hussein saw how necessary he had made himself to the rajah's comfort. Since the date of his appointment until that of annexation, Zahoor-ool Hussein had frequent interviews with Captain Orr, and when, after annexation, that officer was appointed to the district of Mohumdee, in a civil capacity, these interveiws became necessarily very frequent; but, on every occasion, Zahoor-ool Hussein was loud in his expression of gratitude, and appeared ever to consider himself most deeply indebted to his benefactor.

The rebel durbar at Lucknow had now assumed the reins of government; chuckledars and nazims (collectors of revenue) had been appointed to the districts; and orders, very stringent, were issued to all talookdars or landholders in Oude, to present themselves at Lucknow, either personally or through their vakeels, bringing with them as many as possible of their armed retainers to the aid and support of the rebel sepoys now wholly occupied in mad and desperate efforts to crush the garrison in the Lucknow Residency. Zahoor-ool Hussein was selected by Lonee Sing to represent his master at Lucknow. Towards the end of July, he left Mithowlee, with 300 of Lonee Sing's armed followers. But before his departure, and from the time that our people had sought refuge at Mithowlee, never once did Zahoor-ool Hussein endeavour to mitigate the misery in which he saw them plunged, and although he visited them on two occasions, it was merely to give utterance to what he knew was false, or to raise hopes which he also knew the rajah had not the slightest intention of realizing. He had now fairly thrown off all allegiance to the British Government, and the representative of the rajah himself was proceeding to the capital to swell with his followers the ranks of the rebel army. A conversation, however, took place before his departure, between Zahoor-ool Hussein and Lonee Sing, which it is important to note. The vakeel inquired of his master whether on his arrival at Lucknow any mention was to be made at the durbar of the presence at Mithowlee of the Europeans. He was told that unless his master, the rajah, could derive some decided advantage by the disclosure, it was not to be made, but that should the rebel government offer any inducement for his doing so, the rajah would willingly forward his prisoners to Lucknow. This conversation was faithfully reported to Captain Orr by one Mehndee Hussein, one of the inferior karindas of the rajah, who had given several proofs of kindness towards the captives. It was then towards the latter end of July, that Zahoor-ool

Hussein left Mithowlee for Lucknow. On the 6th August, towards evening, Lonee Sing sent word to his captives that he had received positive information that troops were on their way to Mithowlee from Lucknow, with orders to demand the persons of the Europeans under his protection, and that their safety required that they should leave the fort of Kutcheanee immediately, and take refuge once more in the jungles. Of the five Passees appointed by the rajah to watch over his victims, Captain Orr (whose long residence in Oude had made him well acquainted with all the habits and customs of its inhabitants) had succeeded in gaining over two to his own cause. Suspecting treachery, one of these Passees was, on the receipt of the rajah's message, immediately, but secretly, despatched to gain intelligence; he soon returned and stated that troops had actually reached within one day's march of Mithowlee, that they numbered about 250 men, and belonged to five different regiments.* Matters had, to all appearance, now evidently come to a crisis; the rajah had commenced his work of treachery. Zahoor-ool Hussein

* This precaution of selecting men from different regiments was taken in order to remove, as much as possible, all fears of the captives winning the men over to their own interests, which, perhaps, it was thought, might have occurred had men from one regiment only been sent.

had almost immediately, on his arrival at Lucknow, divulged the whole truth, and had urged the durbar to send out a force to escort the hated Europeans to Lucknow. It will naturally be asked, why was the rajah anxious to remove our people from Kutcheanee to the jungles, as since he was determined to sacrifice them to his own benefit, he could as easily have betrayed them whilst in the fort as in the jungle? The answer is easily given: with that vile cunning so common to men of his country and class, he hoped to mask the real motive of his conduct by subsequently, if occasion required, asserting that although by sending his guests to the jungle, he had done his utmost to conceal and save them, yet the presence of a large body of regular troops rendered all his precautions of no avail, and he was constrained to give up those whom he could no longer defend, and thus whilst from the rebel durbar he should reap applause and reward, he should at the same time be screened from all the evil consequences of his conduct should the British once more rule the country. On the night then of the 6th, at ten o'clock, our party left with aching hearts their retreat at Kutcheanee, and proceeded on foot, of course, once more to the jungle. They passed the dismal hours of the night in an opening for the reasons once before mentioned. The guard of Passees were whispering amongst themselves, evidently very earnestly; their conversation was partially overheard by one of the servants, who together with Purwannee, had remained faithful. This servant reported to Captain Orr that he suspected that all was not right, and that foul play was being contemplated. Captain Orr immediately sent for one of the Passees, who revealed the whole truth, saying that the rajah had sent him to the troops to give them information of the whereabouts of the captives, and to guide them to the place of concealment. Will it be believed that 250 men were afraid to accomplish the mission on which they had been sent? They were actually afraid to encounter our small party, expecting to meet with a desperate resistance, and yet such was according to the report of the Passee actually the case—report subsequently verified by the result; for the troops returned empty-handed to Lucknow in September, not having dared, notwithstanding all the remonstrances of the rajah, to penetrate the dreaded jungle. Faithful to his own line of diabolical conduct, he himself refused to make over the captives to the sepoys, who had frequently desired him to do so.

A sad and fearful time was it indeed to our poor people from August 6th, the date of their departure from Kutcheanee, until October 20th, and no pen can give an adequate description of their many and great sufferings. Ladies accustomed to the usual luxuries of life, two delicate little children, one but three years of age, a beautiful little blue-eyed creature, poor little Sophia Christian, whose thoughts constantly reverted to her mother, and who saddened the hearts of her companions by asking them where that beloved mother was; the other, Captain Orr's own daughter Louisa, a little older, who bore up with all the dreadful trials and privations to which she, with her companions, was subjected, with astonishing patience and resignation, and lastly, four men already weakened in mind and body. Such was the party constrained to pass day after day during this long interval, exposed in a dismal jungle to the heat of the day, only tempered with the torrents of rain which in this season of the year are of such frequent occurrence: sickness had commenced to prostrate our people; the dreadful jungle-fever had shown itself; the servants could no longer attend to the wants of their master, and the ladies were forced to cook for the whole party. Small thin choppers made of the jungle grass and broad leaves, had indeed been erected as a protection from the rain, but this protection was but a partial and ineffectual one.

A small supply of quinine and of other medicines was obtained from Captain Hearsey's party, but had arrived in a damaged state; still it was gratefully and thankfully received.

On the 26th of August, a letter reached Captain Orr from Captain Gordon, deputy-assistant adjutant-general at Cawnpore. This letter gave a detailed account of the horrible massacre at Cawnpore, but it also gave the cheering news of the shortly expected arrival of British troops from England, and, above all, of the march on Lucknow of the combined forces of Generals Outram and Havelock. Captain Gordon spoke confidently of the expected result of the operations so soon to be undertaken by our troops; he told Captain Orr that he hoped that, ere long, we should be masters of Lucknow, and that he should have the pleasure of shaking hands with him. Such were that gallant officer's hopes, and such were the hopes, as far as Lucknow was concerned, that filled the hearts of every soul that composed that force. They had a noble object in view; the fate of the brave and glorious garrison of Lucknow hung on a thread, and the awful vow muttered by the soldiers over the dreadful tomb of our countrywomen at Cawnpore was to be fulfilled. Every energy was strained, and all were eager to avenge the cruel death of those that had already fallen, and to save those still in such great jeopardy. How often was that letter read, and read again, laid down but to be once more taken up; and how was the hand that had penned the cheering lines blessed by the grateful hearts to whom, amidst the dreadful gloom, one ray of hope had been conveyed!

We will not dwell any longer on the interval which elapsed between the 6th of August and 20th of October,—an interval filled with hopes and fears, misery and distress. On the 19th of September, 1857, the army under Generals Havelock and Outram crossed the Ganges at Cawnpore; and on the 20th, during a halt made to allow the baggage to be crossed over, a letter was received from Captain Orr by Brigadier-General Neil. This letter was immediately handed over by General Neil to General Outram. An answer returned to it, enclosing a purwanna signed by the General in his capacity of chief commissioner of Oude, to the address of Lonee Sing, instructing him to take the greatest care possible of the Europeans under his charge, and giving him the promise of a very high reward if he should succeed in screening them from danger. Sir James also informed Lonee Sing that he was at the head of an army marching against

Lucknow, and that, after the capture of the city, an European detachment should be sent to Mithowlee to escort the refugees there to Lucknow. A letter was also addressed to Captain Orr by his eldest brother, then with Sir James's camp, enclosing one to Lonee Sing on the all-important subject of those under his care, pointing out to him the advantage that would accrue to him were he faithful to his trust; and, on the contrary, the dreadful punishment that would await him should he prove treacherous. The letter received by Brigadier-General Neil was brought to camp by Purwanee, who was also the bearer of the answers which reached Mithowlee on the 26th of September. The rajah received the General's purwanna in silence, and made to his captives no observations regarding it.

In the meanwhile important events had taken place at Lucknow. Generals Havelock and Outram had, with their troops, forced their way into the Residency. The undertaking was a most desperate one, and could scarcely have been attempted, had not the object in view been one of such vital importance; and although that object was not then and there gained, and the relieving force was itself besieged, yet its presence within the walls of the Lucknow Residency cheered the weary hearts of the long-beleaguered garrison. A new stimulus was given to all, fresh defences were thrown up, sallies were made, and several of the enemy's guns that most annoyed the besieged were captured; in short, though not then relieved, the garrison was fairly saved. But, however, General Outram's design to send an escort to Mithowlee was most unfortunately defeated; communication with the world outside was kept up with the greatest difficulty; and, in fact, important despatches alone were, at enormous expense, conveyed at irregular intervals to Cawnpore. This will explain why it was impossible to communicate with those at Mithowlee, to which place our narrative must now be carried back. It has already been stated that the detachment sent from Lucknow, at the instigation of the villain Zahoor-ool Hussein, had returned, empty handed, to Lucknow in September. On its arrival at the capital, Zahoor-ool Hussein, disappointed at not seeing his victims brought in, himself started for Mithowlee under a promise, on oath, to the rebel government that he would shortly return with those his master had so solemnly sworn to protect. Zahoor-ool Hussein went so far as to ask the durbar whether he should bring the captives alive, or whether their heads only were required. He was ordered to bring them in alive.

Zahoor-ool Hussein reached Mithowlee one or two days before the rajah received General Outram's purwanna. It so happened that this purwanna was put into Captain Orr's hands at the time that Zahoor-ool Hussein had been chosen to pay a visit to the captives. He, as well as the rajah, heard all the account given by Purwanee, read the General's purwanna, but retired silently.

All was again quiet at Mithowlee for some days after the arrival of the villain Zahoor-ool Hussein. The rajah was watching the course of events; before taking any decisive step, he wished to see the result of the operations at Lucknow. How cruelly and coolly was all calculated, and how cautiously did the villains carry on their fatal plot! They were soon convinced that the balance preponderated in favour of the rebel government, and that the days of the English were numbered. Preparations were therefore made to send the captives to Lucknow, and on the morning of the 20th October, 1857, a party of 300 of Lonee Sing's men, armed with matchlocks and swords, entered the jungle. Zahoor-ool Hussein was himself present, but kept at a short distance. Captain Orr had with him a pistol and a gun. The first act of the ruffians was to seize upon these arms; this was sufficient to throw a light upon their designs. Our party were all suffering from fever, which attacked them every other day; they were besides without clothes, except the rags that covered them, without shoes, and, above all, without any protection for the head; and in this state they were ordered to follow the men. In vain did they ask where they were to be taken—no answer was returned, but the order was again brutally given to move on. Sergeant-major Morton begged permission to take with him a piece of cloth which had served him as a carpet—this was refused. Mrs. Orr also wished to take with her a sheet, with which to cover her head as well as that of her little daughter; but one of the cowardly ruffians accompanied his refusal with a blow which levelled her with the ground. It is useless to attempt to describe the scene now before us; and could an accurate account be given, it would be one of a nature too harrowing. Let us then hurry on. Our party escorted by 300 men walked or rather dragged themselves on to the edge of the jungle, where two of the common country two-wheeled carts awaited them; they were told to mount, and the party proceeded to a village, distant about a mile or a mile and a half. Here they halted, for another scene of brutal cruelty was to be enacted at this place. A native blacksmith soon made his appearance, bringing with him heavy fetters. Zahoor-ool Hussein was determined to fill the cup of revenge to the full; with savage foresight he had prepared everything; no delay was to occur; the gentlemen of the party were to be laden with irons at once. Alas! at this indignity the mind of poor Barnes received a shock from which it never recovered. Morton, at the dreaded sight of the fetters, fell into a frightful convulsive fit, from which he with difficulty recovered, through the slight attentions which could be paid to him by his fellow-captives. Death at one moment seemed ready to terminate his sufferings; the operation of fixing the fetters was suspended, but to be savagely renewed as soon as symptoms of returning life appeared. The heaviest pair of fetters were destined by Zahoor-ool Hussein for Captain Orr. His wife begged that the indignity might be dispensed with, falling down on her knees before the monsters; but a rude laugh was returned to all her supplications. The iron was fixed, and the order for the march given, Zahoor-ool Hussein ordering all the movements. Will it be believed that the piece of string which prisoners usually attach to the upper ring or joint of the fetters, to enable them with a little more ease to keep the irons in a position favourable to motion, was, with a refinement of cruelty, refused? The march lasted from the 20th to the 26th October; each day the sad procession started at 8 o'clock A.M., and continued with slight interruption until evening closed in.

The sufferings from the sun were dreadful—a raging thirst tormented the poor captives, and no water was allowed to allay it. Food, such as it was, was thrown (let this expression be taken literally) to them at irregular intervals, and often did it happen that it was midnight ere they received the nauseous pittance. But if the bodily suffering was so great, the moral suffering was still greater; at every village passed, the poor prisoners were exhibited to the wondering villagers.

What a triumph to the gaolers to hold in their power those, to whom a short time since, they had been accustomed to pay implicit respect, and whose word had been considered law! what a triumph to be able now to speak to them in the tones of the most cowardly insolence, and to load them with the most cruel indignity! We must not fail to note the order of the march: 150 of the armed force marched in front, with a cannon always kept ready for action, and 150 brought up the rear, further protected by another cannon, the prisoners in the centre. On approaching the capital on the 26th October, 1858, the party was reinforced by three regiments of the line, and a swarm of cavalry. The Residency was carefully avoided, for beleaguered and besieged as it was, it was still an object of dread, and a circuitous road was chosen to conduct the prisoners to the palace, the now notorious Kaiser Bagh. Before reaching this building, Captain Orr recognized a large detachment of sepoys, formerly belonging to his own regiment. The detachment was drawn up in one of the streets of the city, and as the prisoners' carts passed by, many of the men were seen to cry violently.

It will be remembered that it was a guard of this very corps that saved their former commandant's life at the massacre at Nourungabad of the Shahjehanpore fugitives. At some short distance from the Kaiser Bagh, the captives were made to dismount from the carts; they had hardly done so, when they were completely surrounded by a dense crowd, and progress was rendered most difficult. The reader will imagine the dreadful position of the captives, rudely and insultingly stared at by thousands exulting in the sight. Captain Orr snatched up his little daughter in his arms, expecting every moment to see her torn to pieces by the crowd. Mr. Barnes performed the same kind office towards little Sophia Christian. The thirst which had so long tormented the poor prisoners had now become intolerable, and in agony the ladies shrieked out for water. It was denied to them, until Munnoo Khan, the paramour of the Begum, whose son, Birjees Kudr, had been placed on the throne, and who, from the Kaiser Bagh, had been watching the progress of the captives, ordered water to be given to them; it was brought, but in such a vile vessel, that even situated as they were, the ladies refused to pollute their mouths with it. At last the agony was over—the party reached the smaller entrance of the Kaiser Bagh, the door was suddenly opened, the prisoners admitted, and it was as suddenly closed. The hated crowd was excluded; but seeing themselves separated from their prey, they raised a fearful yell and dispersed. Poor Sir Mountstewart Jackson had suffered much from frequent attacks of fever and ague; nature was fairly worn out, and it was a melancholy sight to see his frame utterly and hopelessly reduced to the last extremity by distress, sickness, and misery. On entering the Kaiser Bagh, he fell down in a swoon; orders were given to some menials to place him on a charpoy.

The whole party were now taken to their place of

confinement, in a small miserable room in one of the numerous out-houses of the Kaiser Bagh, attached to the stabling, a guard of twelve men in the Ukhturree Regiment was posted at the door as a watch. During the first day of their confinement, one Meer Wajid Alee, of whom more afterwards, was present with the guard. He had the humanity to give to the prisoners the dinner prepared for himself. At midnight the place of confinement was changed for another one more roomy, and better in all respects, the guard was considerably increased, and always kept their swords drawn.

To render the subsequent portion of our narrative more intelligible, we will give a hurried sketch of the state of affairs at the Oude rebel durbar. Twelve regiments had been raised by the British Government on annexation; of these regiments the greater number had previously belonged to the Oude service. This force, including also several regiments of cavalry, was styled the Oude Irregular Force. At the commencement of the siege of Lucknow, it was by these troops, composed by most part of Oude men, that the claims of the king were made in the person of a boy ten or twelve years of age, his name Birjees Kudr, the supposed son of the ex-king, Wajid Alee, but the real offspring of one Munnoo Khan. The mother of this boy had originally been a dancing girl, with whom Munnoo Khan, then holding a subordinate charge in the royal cook-room, had formed an intimacy. The king, hearing of the girl's beauty, admitted her to the number of his mahuls, under the title of "Huzrut Mahul." She received a handsome allowance, with a large establishment, of which she appointed Munnoo Khan the darogah or superintendent. The former intimacy was still, though secretly, carried on, and resulted in the birth of the boy Birjees Kudr. On the elevation of Birjees Kudr to the throne, or rather on his being created Wazier of Oude—for his authority was at first held subordinate to that of the emperor of Delhi—his mother and Munnoo Khan enjoyed an amount of power, checked only by the caprices of the troops to whom their elevation had been due. Munnoo Khan was a man of no talent whatsoever, and alike wanting in that courage, both moral and physical, so requisite in a person in the critical position which he now held.

As to the Meer Wajid Alee, whom we have already had occasion to name, he held with regard to another Begum, known as the Sooltan Mahul, the same position as did Munnoo Khan with regard to the Huzrut Mahul, *nominally* the darogah of her household, in *reality* living with her on the most intimate terms, the king the dupe of both these women. Between Meer Wajid Alee and Munnoo Khan, however, exists this great difference; the former is of a respectable family of Syuds, the latter of low origin; the former has received what amongst the Mahomedans of Central India is considered a good education, the latter is almost ignorant of even the art of reading and writing his own language. Wajid Alee had charge of the financial arrangements of the durbar.

Two or three days after the arrival at Lucknow of the English prisoners, this event became known to the Lucknow garrison. Some of the British scouts had already given information that certain English prisoners had been brought to Lucknow from the district, but their information was vague. It was, however, shortly confirmed by one of Rajah Maun Sing's Moonshees, who presented himself within the British entrenchment, the bearer of a letter from his master to Sir James Outram. This person gave all particulars; and through him, with the sanction of the general, communication was held with the captives; a letter was received written by Captain Orr and signed by all his companions, stating that Meer Wajid Alee, Munnoo Khan, and Maun Sing were showing them kindness, and that their fetters had been removed. Maun Sing himself wrote to the general and also to Captain Orr's brothers, both of whom were in the Lucknow garrison, that he would exert himself to the best to save the captives. Although Rajah Maun Sing had in his letter somewhat exaggerated the extent of his kind offices towards them, and had given the general and Captain Orr's brothers to understand that he had caused the fetters to be removed, yet it was subsequently discovered that it was to Meer Wajid Alee that the gentlemen were indebted for this act of kindness.

Maun Sing certainly rendered signal service in facilitating communication with Wajid Alee; and here let us state once for all, that the behaviour of this man was from the very first invariably kind and considerate, and above all, full of respect. It appears from his conversation with Mrs. Orr, that he had endeavoured to prevent the massacre in the city of nineteen persons (amongst whom was Miss Georgiana Jackson, the sister of Sir Mountstewart) on the memorable day of the entrance into Lucknow of the troops under Generals Havelock and Outram; un fortunately they were in the custody of the Delhi troops, then under the complete influence of the moulvie,* and to have spoken or acted openly in

* Note by Captain Hutchinson.—This was the moulvie alluded to before at Fyzabad.

their favour would certainly have caused the death of Meer Wajid Alee. From the 26th October to the 16th November, the prisoners received frequent visits from Munnoo Khan. His object was to persuade Sir Mountstewart Jackson and Captain Orr to write, the one to his uncle, Mr. C. C. Jackson, the other to Sir James Outram, that the durbar was willing to release the prisoners and to allow the garrison to leave the city unmolested should the British consent to abandon Oude entirely. Both officers refused to be the channel of communication of this proposition, persuaded as they were that should the British, on the faith of the rebels, leave the Residency, the Cawnpore tragedy would again be enacted. Failing in this purpose, Munnoo Khan, through one of his agents, sent word to the officers, that since they refused to write they must head the troops in their assaults on the beleaguered garrison, cast shells, &c. This the officers indignantly refused to do, and plainly told Munnoo Khan that nothing could induce them to join the rebel army against their own countrymen. On hearing this Munnoo Khan left the room and mentioned the circumstance to one of the men of the guard, who ferociously made a fearful sign, passing his finger across his throat; this sign did not pass unobserved by Mrs. Orr and her husband, who felt that the last hour was come, and told their poor companions to prepare for the worst: but it did not suit Munnoo Khan then to carry the threat into execution.

Everything tended to make the position of the prisoners as dreadful as possible. The nature of the feelings towards them of their gaolers had been sufficiently manifest; and their feeling would, it was feared, but be increased by the refusal of the officers to act in a manner dishonourable to themselves. As to their personal comforts, they were but scanty. They received food indeed, but it was given in small quantities, and only proved sufficient because several of the poor captives were in too sickly a state to partake of it. Poor Sir Mountstewart was wasting away. Morton, for days together, refused to touch food of any kind. Barnes was all but insensible to all external events. Captain Orr was so changed, that even those who in Oude had for years past been intimately acquainted with him, could not recognize him. If such was the fearful change that had taken place in the person of the gentlemen, how much more startling must it not have been with regard to the ladies, Mrs. Orr and Miss Jackson! Their clothes, even in the jungles, had already long since been in tatters; they were now entirely in rags. Their hair was completely matted, deprived as they were of combs and brushes, or, in fact, of all those little articles of toilet so necessary to ensure cleanliness. In a word, body and mind alike suffered, the sufferings of the one, in fact, increasing the suffering of the other. The poor little children, too—what a fate was theirs!

We have already stated that, through the kindness of Wajid Alee, the fetters had been removed from the legs of the gentlemen. The moulvie had by some means been informed of this, and he sent one of his men to ascertain exactly the fact. Fortunately, Wajid Alee heard of the circumstance, and, bribing handsomely the spy, induced him to report to the moulvie that the fetters had not been discontinued.

We have nothing new to relate until the arrival of Sir Colin Campbell to effect the relief of the besieged garrison. Some letters, it is true, had been sent by Captain Orr to the Residency, and answers returned, but some of the former only reached their destination long after date. In the meanwhile, during all this dreary period, alternate hopes and fears had been entertained at the Residency regarding the probable fate of the captives. General Outram wrote in strong language to Rajah Maun Sing, enforcing upon him the necessity of saving the lives of the prisoners, and assuring him that this act alone would convince him .that the rajah was sincere, on his protestations of fidelity. Indeed, Maun Sing wrote on several occasions to the general on his own account, but invariably received the assurance that the rescue from captivity and death of the prisoners was the *sine quâ non* of his ultimately receiving pardon. But alas! it was doomed that the warmest and most earnest hopes were to be disappointed. Wajid Alee had latterly been obliged to discontinue his visits to the captives. He had for some time past been, by the fiend moulvie, suspected of showing too much kindness to the prisoners; and so bitter was the feeling of the moulvie on this account towards Wajid Alee, that the latter was obliged to conceal himself during four days in the city. Fortunately, Munnoo Khan could not dispense with his services, and plainly told the chiefs of the rebel army, that unless Wajid Alee was protected from the menaces of the moulvie, and allowed to resume his duties, he (Munnoo Khan) could not carry on his own. Wajid Alee was consequently, under a most solemn promise of protection, allowed to return to the Kaiser Bagh; but of course he was obliged to be very cautious in his rare interviews with the captives. On the 14th November, heavy firing was heard in the suburbs of the city. The guard placed over the prisoners immediately got under arms, and the jemadar, or native officer in command, was heard to give strict orders not to allow either Munnoo Khan or Meer Wajid Alee to communicate with the prisoners. This day, and that of the 15th, were passed in the most wretched anxiety. Great tumult and uproar reigned in the Kaiser Bagh; so great, indeed, that it prevented the prisoners from hearing the cannonading of Sir Colin's advancing army. On the 16th November, a large body of men of the 71st Native Infantry rushed towards the room where the captives were lodged. They were completely equipped, wearing the cross-belts over their own native clothes. On their arrival, the former guard withdrew; and all the inmates of that wretched room were ordered, in language too brutal to be repeated, to rise and come forward. Not a word was spoken by our poor countrymen, who rose with some difficulty. We cannot describe the solemn and awful scene, and with harrowed feelings we will drop the veil over what is perhaps too sacred to be revealed. Another person, evidently in authority, now appeared and whispered some orders into the ear of the man commanding the party of the 71st. This order it was soon discovered was to leave the ladies where they were, and to drag the officers away. All felt in that dreadful hour that the fiat had gone forth; the poor children uttered a loud shriek, as if their tender reason was about to abandon them; a solemn adieu was said by Sir Mountstewart Jackson and Captain Orr to those they had loved so much; cords were produced, the prisoners, undaunted in spirit even at this dreadful moment, allowed themselves calmly to be bound, and soon were seen no more. A rattle of musketry was heard by those who had been left behind, although its fearful tale was not then understood by them; nor even was it revealed for some time afterwards, as the native guard persisted, when questioned on the subject, in saying that some native prisoners had been put to death, and that the English captives were still in the custody of the 71st Regiment. Whether this false statement was made from motives of pity, or from some other reason, it is difficult to say. It was on the 7th January, 1858, that Wajid Alee, being repeatedly interrogated by Mrs. Orr, disclosed the truth, adding that the crime had been committed at the instigation of the moulvie. But to continue—the jemadar of the guard which had been placed over them was in the habit, now and then, of leaving his charges to assist in pointing the guns of one of the numerous batteries of the

Kaiser Bagh—he was considered a good shot, and was rewarded by a donation of 500 rupees for having, by a round shot, knocked down the British flag which Sir Colin's victorious troops had placed on one of the turrets of the Khoor Sheid Munzil,* and which was known to the English residents of Lucknow under the designation of the mess-house of her Majesty's 32nd Regiment. This jemadar was of a brutal disposition, and was killed at his battery by one of our shots on the 15th November. He was succeeded by another jemadar, who, though bad enough, was still a little less cruel than his predecessor. After the enactment of the scene just described as having occurred on the 16th, the ladies had apparently been forgotten, and for two whole days no food had been sent to them—a few morsels of dry chuppatees, the remnants of former repasts, had fortunately been carefully preserved, and these, moistened with water, were now and then given to the children when oppressed with hunger. At last the jemadar reported to his superior officer, that either the prisoners must be fed, or he must be relieved of his charge; a person styling himself "adjutant," came to verify the jemadar's statement. Finding the account had not been exaggerated, he

* *Khoor Sheid*—the sun; *Munzil*—house, edifice.

gave one rupee to the jemadar with which to procure food. Rice and dall were now given to the ladies, and this food was cooked by the camp followers in the British service, who had fallen into the hands of the enemy. Preparations were now being made for the masterly operations by which the garrison of Lucknow was to be relieved. A sham bombarding of the Kaiser Bagh was commenced. The house in which the ladies was confined was not secure from the effects of the iron hail, and the guard, fearing probably for their own safety, were seriously thinking of cruelly getting rid of their charge; but monstrous as they were, they one by one refused to strike the first blow. At this juncture their good genius, Wajid Alee, once more appeared to the aid of the ladies, and he persuaded the jemadar to conduct his prisoners to their former abode, the stables: much confusion existed, and Wajid Alee seized upon the opportunity thus afforded to renew his visits, although these visits were few and far between, and made under disguise.

The Lucknow garrison had now been relieved; women and children, sick and wounded, had all most providentially been extricated from their perilous situation, and the two forces, the relieving and the relieved, marched on to the Alumbagh.

Sir Colin hastened on to the relief of Cawnpore, then invested by the Nana and the Gwalior troops. Sir James Outram, with a very inadequate force, was to hold the Alumbagh, a position which was considered a most important one. Great was the joy, at Lucknow, of the rebels, as our forces abandoned the city; in their madness, they thought they were delivered for ever of their hated enemies, and that the force left by Sir Colin at Alumbagh merely waited for reinforcements to join the Commander-in-Chief; not reflecting that, had a complete abandonment of the province been finally determined upon, Sir James Outram's force would naturally have either at once joined the body of the army, or at least have at once followed it; but they were blinded. In their mad joy, they at once released nearly two hundred native prisoners; but this error, on their part, was most providential, as our captive countrywomen were for a time forgotten. It was with an aching heart that they were told by the jailors that the British had left the Residency; the last faint hope of delivery seemed destroyed for ever; and their sorrow was increased by a sad event which occurred on or about the 24th of November. Poor little Sophie Christian had, during the long period which our narrative embraces, been struggling with sickness and hardship; her poor little frame had been shattered by repeated attacks of fever and dysentery; but although she had appeared latterly to rally, yet nature was completely exhausted, and on the day alluded to, the 24th of November, the poor little angel laid her down and slept. Death passed his hand gently over her; her beautiful eyes closed softly, as if in gentle sleep; and before her companions could perceive the change, her infant spirit had fled for ever from the scene of danger and of misery. Through the kindness of a man of the guard, himself the father of a large family, and upon whom Mrs. Orr had imposed a solemn oath, and also by bribing another person to lend his services in the performance of the sad ceremony, Mrs. Orr and Miss Jackson had the melancholy satisfaction of knowing that, during the dark hours of the ensuing night, the remains of the little girl were carefully confided to the earth. This event naturally cast a gloom over minds already wrung to the utmost by apprehension, anxiety, and grief. Day after day passed away without bringing any comfort—indeed, perhaps, more painfully than the preceding one. Their food, instead of being cooked separately, was but a small portion of the general mess prepared for their native prisoners; and coarse native clothes, already worn, were given in lieu of the tattered remnants of their English garments.

Captain Orr's brother had been attached to General Sir J. Outram's staff, in the intelligence department, and, after many efforts, they succeeded in establishing communication with Wajid Alee, and, through his kindness, with the prisoners, to whom they were enabled to send secretly and with extreme caution a small supply of the most necessary medicines, and of tea. A few letters were received by either party, but very irregularly, and at long intervals. Communication was also held from the Alumbagh with Meer Wajid Alee, and with Maun Sing's vakeel; for Maun Sing himself had left Lucknow for his own residence at Shahgunge, or at least had pretended to do so.

It is impossible to appreciate the kindness of General Outram, in all his constant endeavours, by threats and promises, by offers of several rewards, to secure the safety of the prisoners; and to him, under Providence, are our countrywomen most deeply indebted for their subsequent release. Wajid Alee gave a solemn promise, to effect, if possible, the deliverance of the captives; he made this promise not only to General Outram, but confirmed it in the presence of the ladies by a sacred oath, swearing on the heads of his own children. This is the most binding of all oaths amongst natives. But how, amidst the many intricate passages of the Kaiser Bagh, exposed from every side to the gaze of the soldiery crowded within its walls, could the prisoners be withdrawn? As a preliminary step, Wajid Alee, through his influence with Munnoo Khan, representing that the health of the captives was affected, removed them to a house nearer to one of the main roads of the city, and also, as much as possible, spread in the city the report that the ladies had been killed by a shot from the British entrenchments.

One Anunt Ram, the vakeel of Rajah Maun Sing, sometimes accompanied Wajid Alee in his visits to the captive ladies, and it was about the month of January that Anunt Ram suggested the idea of secretly carrying away Mrs. Orr's little daughter, Louisa, and rescuing her from captivity. Wajid Alee entered warmly into the plans proposed to be adopted by Anunt Ram. Food was sent very irregularly to the natives; and in fact, during a temporary absence from his home of Wajid Alee, it was withheld altogether, under pretext of putting a stop to this evil, but in reality with a far different object in view. Wajid Alee engaged for the ladies the services of a native woman, a resident of Lucknow.

This woman was a rough, masculine creature, possessed of much ready wit and courage, and admirably adapted for the part she was destined to play. The native physician of the court was a kind-hearted man, and his conduct on more than one occasion showed that he was touched at the sight of the sufferings of our countrywomen. Wajid Alee sought his assistance, and easily persuaded him to report to the durbar that the child was dangerously ill, and that he had no hopes of her recovery. This report was sent in daily; but it was necessary also to gain over the commandant of the corps, which furnished the guard over the prisoners; this man, however, at once refused to connive at the escape of the little prisoner, and Wajid Alee was plunged into no little anxiety at having been obliged to divulge his secret to this person, who would in all probability have made the whole plot public, had he not been restrained by the fact of his owing his own appointment to the kindness of Wajid Alee. Although the scheme had failed, yet Wajid Alee did not despair of success through other means. He allowed several days to pass apparently in inactivity, he treated the commandant with the greatest kindness, but in the meanwhile he adroitly persuaded Munnoo Khan to employ the commandant's regiment in levying contributions of money (then urgently required) on the principal inhabitants of Lucknow. For this purpose all the guards of the regiment were withdrawn from their posts, and relieved by men from other regiments. This arrangement, it will easily be understood, pleased the commandant vastly, as it afforded him and his men an opportunity of enriching themselves. Having succeeded thus far, Wajid Alee took care that the new, or relieving guard over the prisoners should be composed of men of his own choice, who received orders not to allow any person to communicate with the prisoners, and if questioned as to the nature of their duty, to state that they were placed as a guard over the stables. The hakeem, or physician, once more made his daily reports to the durbar of the bad state of the little girl's health. The commandant, suspecting that Wajid Alee was again favouring her escape, reported the circumstance to Munnoo Khan, who immediately sent a person, by name Ally Jan, to ascertain whether little Louisa was in reality as ill as reported. Ally Jan was on terms of friendship with both Munnoo Khan and Wajid Alee, but more especially with the latter, to whom he constantly reported all that occurred at the durbar and at the councils of the rebel chiefs of the army, to the latter of which Wajid Alee was not admitted. It is needless to say that Ally Jan made a favourable report. The hakeem now reported that the supposed invalid had ceased to exist. The guard was only bribed by Wajid Alee, its commanding officer himself receiving 300 rupees. On the eighth day all was ready—the hands, feet, and legs of the little girl had been coloured so as to resemble in tint those of a native child. She was covered as much as possible with a cloth, and confided to the care of the woman before mentioned. To give as great an appearance of reality as possible to the whole transaction, Wajid Alee had instructed the jemadar of the guard to depute one of his men to demand of Munnoo Khan the money necessary to defray the expenses of the burial. The woman, accompanied by the jemadar himself, now left the place, carrying the precious burden on her back, bemoaning and lamenting her pretended loss with all the gestures and usages of native women on such occasions. Her acting was perfect, and with great presence of mind she passed all the guards without attracting suspicion; she was guided, though very secretly, by the jemadar to Rajah Maun Sing's city residence, whence shortly afterwards she was removed by Anunt Ram to one of Maun Sing's forts, and thence, eventually, after the lapse of several days, to the British camp at the Alumbagh; but the passage through the city and the journey to the fort in the district were not accomplished without incurring great risk at Chinhut (a short distance from Lucknow). Anunt Ram and his party had to pass through the camp of the moulvie, who had suddenly and without the knowledge of Anunt Ram encamped at that place. The moulvie's troops challenged the party, and it required all the skill of Anunt Ram to satisfy the questions put to him. It would be difficult to describe the feeling of the mother when the moment of separation had arrived—nothing but the ardent desire to see her child safe from all danger, could have induced her to overcome all doubts and fears, and to confide her beloved child to the care of strangers.

General Sir James Outram had now left Alumbagh to take command of a strong division on the other side of the Goomtee. The bombardment of the city had commenced in right earnest. During three days the ladies were exposed to much danger, the shells falling near, and indeed on one occasion on the very building in which they were lodged. Wajid

16

Alee consequently obtained permission to remove his charge to another house in the city: to effect this the ladies were both placed in one doolee, which, however, had not proceeded far when it was stopped by the sentry at the grand doorway of the Kaiser Bagh. The soldier said he would not allow the doolee to pass without seeing the hands and feet of those inside. This was an anxious and critical moment, but Wajid Alee, foreseeing everything, had bribed an old chobdar of the former time, a man who had well known Captain Orr, from whom he had frequently received presents, to accompany the ladies. As soon as the sentry had uttered his wish to examine the hands and feet of the occupants of the doolee, the old chobdar immediately came forward, and with ready answer told him that the doolee contained one of the favourite begums, who was proceeding to pay her devotions at one of the holy shrines in the city, and that she would return to the palace the next morning. The old man pretended great indignation at the sentry having had the audacity to threaten to remove the purdah of the conveyance, and in fact spoke and managed so well, that the bewildered sepoys allowed the doolee to pass without further opposition clear of the Kaiser Bagh. Many dangers still awaited our party whilst passing through streets crowded with lawless and independent soldiers, but Providence guided them, and they reached their destination in safety, followed by the guard, supposed by the passers-by to be one of honour accompanying a native lady of high rank. Of course the confusion reigning in the city at the time favoured the passage of the party; but still the new abode was not secure against the messengers of death hurled by the British against the doomed city, and Wajid Alee removed to yet another house in the suburbs occupied by the Sultan Mahul, and Wajid Alee's wife and children, as well as by his brother-in-law's family. Here the ladies were most kindly received, clothes provided for them, and all their wants, as much as possible, attended to. The British, already masters of the Kaiser Bagh and of the principal buildings in the city, were driving the enemy from its outskirts, a portion of which was still held by the moulvie. The monster had long suspected Wajid Alee of being friendly to the English, and his object was to seize him as he had seized Shurfood Dowlah, the minister, under the rebel administration. Communication with the British camp, though often interrupted, was still kept up with Wajid Allee, who was plunged in the greatest anxiety regarding the safety of the ladies and of his own large family.

The moulvie had discovered on the 18th March the abode of Wajid Alee, who through his own informants, had been made well aware of the designs of his enemy. The position in which the ladies now found themselves was most critical, for although the British, as we have before stated, were masters of the principal portions of the city, yet the moulvie with a considerable force still held a position in the suburbs. On the night of the 17th or 18th March, Wajid Alee wrote to Captain Orr's brother, pointing out the extreme danger in which he was placed, and begged assistance without delay. This letter was shown to Sir J. Outram, who communicated, we believe, on the subject with General Macgregor, then with the Gorkha troops most providentially in the neighbourhood of Wajid Alee's house; but the danger was imminent, the moulvie with his men was hourly expected, and no time was to be lost. Wajid Alee begged of Mrs. Orr to write a note, explaining the difficulties and danger by which she was surrounded, to the address of any British officer; this note he should cause to be conveyed to the nearest British post. Mrs. Orr wrote a few lines which were confided to Wajid Alee's brother-in-law. This person, however, had hardly left the house when he encountered a body of Gorkhas under the command of two British officers, Captains MacNeil and Bogle. He immediately explained to them the nature of his errand, and led the way to the house.

The moulvie was already coming in the same direction from another quarter. The officers rushed into the house, and without the loss of a moment placed the ladies in a palanquin: no bearers could be found, but the servants of the officers and some Gorkhas were pressed into the service, and Captain MacNeil, accompanying the palanquin, commenced his perilous journey, leaving Captain Bogle with the Gorkhas to escort Wajid Alee and his family. It must be remembered that Captain MacNeil had to pass through narrow streets entirely devoid of British troops, and about which the enemy were still hovering, and that he might at every moment expect an attack, or at all events a ball from some hidden assassin. Captain MacNeil, however, rushed on, urging and encouraging his party to make the most strenuous efforts. The Char Bagh ravine was reached and crossed, and a little farther General Magregor's camp came in sight; on—on—swiftly was the palanquin borne; the friendly camp is at length gained, and the ladies are safe. It is needless to say how kindly and cordially the ladies were received by General Macgregor and his officers. Every attention was shown to them, and on the next day, the 20th March, they were escorted to General Sir J. Outram's camp, where Mrs. Orr had the inexpressible delight of once more clasping her daughter in her arms.

But we must return to Captain Bogle, the brave companion of Captain MacNeil. With much difficulty and at much risk he succeeded in escorting the whole of Meer Wajid Allee's family to General Macgregor's camp. The difficulty of his enterprise will be better understood by those acquainted with native manners and customs. To these officers our once captive countrywomen are indeed much indebted for the gallantry and presence of mind that they displayed on the occasion, when delay or hesitation would have been fatal. In after years the souvenir of the deed performed by Captains MacNeil and Bogle at Lucknow will not be reckoned as the least among pleasurable reminiscences.

We will now conclude. We have accompanied our countrymen step by step amidst danger and death, and have given to our readers a faithful, and we hope not an uninteresting narrative of what they suffered. Many details have been omitted in order not to clog unnecessarily the statement of more important events.

Let it not be understood that we have intentionally placed Captain Orr and his wife more prominently before our readers than we have done their equally unfortunate and suffering companions. Their intimate knowledge of the country and of its language and customs necessarily, on most occasions, constrained them to take a leading part in their every-day intercourse with the natives. We must, however, make mention of one circumstance, the nature of which cannot but strike the most callous minds, before the final separation of the gentlemen from the ladies in the Kaiser Bagh. Mrs. Orr had occasion to send for some native medicines; they were brought to her wrapped up in a piece of printed paper. On glancing her eyes over it, Mrs. Orr perceived that it was a portion of a leaf of a Bible, and contained the following passage of Isaiah, chap. li., ver. 11: "They shall obtain gladness and joy; and sorrow and mourning shall flee away. I, even I, am He that comforteth you: who art thou, that thou shouldest be afraid of a man that shall die, and of the son of man which shall be made as grass; and forgettest the Lord thy Maker, that hath stretched forth the heavens, and laid down the foundations of the earth; and hast feared continually every day because of the fury of the oppressor, as if he were ready to destroy? and where is the fury of the oppressor? The captive exile hasteneth that he may be loosed, and that he should not die in the pit, nor that——"

(Signed) A. ORR, *Captain*,
Deputy Commissioner.

The accompanying deposition by a Madras servant, and á brief memorandum I drew up on the subject, give allthat is circumstantially known as to the mode of our poor countrymen's death, and also the probable locality where the murder was perpetrated, which according to the foregoing account took place on the 16th November, 1857.

Deposition of Lorgeress, Madrasee, a Christian, native of Belaree, born and bred a Camp-follower.

Came with the force of General Havelock. Was with the troops under General Neil, when that officer was killed, endeavouring to escape with other natives, he rushed unwittingly, as did many others, into a house held by sepoys who seized him at once; he was plundered, and said he was a sweeper.

First took him to Kaiser Bagh, and afterwards to Gisaree Mundee, near the Kaiser Bagh. When Sir Colin Campbell entered Lucknow, the three gentlemen were shot and left lying about one hundred yards outside a gateway of the Kaiser Bagh.

During Sir Colin's first attack the bodies lay there, and after he went away this man and other prisoners were brought out to bury them.

He observed three bodies tied arm to arm, not back to back; one body, a short man, had a Prayer-book in his waistcoat pocket; one body, cannot remember which, had jingal bullet sticking in his left side.

All the bodies had European clothes on, but one body had native shoes on; stockings appeared on all, as the other bodies had shoes on of European make; a leather helmet hat lay near one body.

The short body had no beard; others, cannot remember faces, perfectly black from corruption, as also the hands.

The three bodies lying in a row on their backs, tied arm to arm, looked so black, that I first thought they were natives.

A trench was near, and, according to orders, I aided in helping to untie their arms; we placed them in the trench one over the other, and put the hat and book with them.

The sepoys standing looking on when we arrived to bury the bodies, were joking, and saying to each other, "Who are these men? they must be great men; governors, perhaps;" to which the reply, over and over repeated, was, "Oh yes, this one is

Governor of Madras, that of Bombay, and that of Bengal."

Ground been so altered since, that I cannot recognize the place where they were buried.

Memo.—I went with the Madrasee, who gave the deposition foregoing, and starting from a gateway belonging to the Kaiser Bagh, which he recognized, we, after a long search and conversation with native mistrys, who had apparently seen the last fortifications made, ascertained the spot where probably the house had stood, under the cover of which the Madrasee remembered crouching on his way to inter the bodies, and from which he hoped to trace his next land-mark, a kutcha wall. After clearing away rubbish and digging, we definitely laid bare the foundation of the sought-for house, which exactly corresponded in position, size, and description, as given by the Madrasee, with that of the native mistrys and tindals.

Then came the extreme difficulty of tracing a mud-wall, along which he had gone, until he reached a trench in which the bodies were hastily buried. For a considerable time we traced all the directions of this wall, the existence of which the mistrys quite recollected, but of which now no trace remained. At length we decided on the point it ran to, and from which extreme the Madrasee said the trench lay about thirty feet in the direction of the Chuttur Munzil; but here we were completely and finally foiled: the first day all the mistrys maintained no trench had existed there at all, and the second day, that though some fancied they recollected a trench, yet that it had been completely swallowed up and dug out in the vast ditch or canal, as the natives call it, dug round the Kaiser Bagh palace. In the last fortifications thrown up, I examined the ground very carefully and very disappointedly, for I had felt almost certain of at last finding the bones of our murdered countrymen; but further examination only convinced me more of the extreme probability that their rude grave had been included in the vast ditch, and thus no trace remained. I, however, had the only remaining trench of the enemy which was discernible thoroughly excavated, but found nothing.

The locality of the murder within fifty yards either way I have determined, but for all else can only regret my great want of success.

I would suggest that a plain but well proportioned monument be erected on the spot, which If eel sure is within fifty yards of their last resting-place; this monument should be enclosed by an iron railing, as the site is at the junction of two or three new roads.

For inscription—as it does not appear desirable in so public a place to put up any words tending to perpetuate the ill-feeling between the white man and the black, so it cannot be that our grievous wrong should be entirely unnoticed—I would therefore propose that the names of the fallen be inscribed, with the date as near as can be given, and this simple remark—

"VICTIMS OF 1857."

It will be remembered that in the narrative of Captain John Hearsey, the ladies of his party, with Mr. Carew, got separated from him and other gentlemen, and that this occurred when the whole party was attacked by the Dhowrairah rebels, near the banks of the Chonka river.

It has been ascertained that the unfortunate ladies, with Mr. Carew and the stepson of Sergeant-Major Rodgers, eventually fell into the hands of the Rajah of Dhowrairah, and were sent into Lucknow.

I have ascertained the spot where they were shot by the rebel sepoys, and a suitable monument will be erected to their memory and that of others who perished with them at that place.

The following account, by Meer Wajid Alee, Darogah, is the most complete statement I have been able to get regarding their fate.

The exact date of their foul murder it is impossible to fix, but all accounts appear to point to its having been perpetrated a very few days after the late General Sir Henry Havelock, K.C.B., entered with General Sir James Outram, G.C.B., to relieve the garrison in the Residency.

Translation of a Memorandum furnished by Meer Wajid Alee, Darogah of Lucknow, who saved Mrs. Orr and Miss Jackson.

The following persons were sent to Lucknow by the Rajah of Dhowrairah, under the escort of three hundred men, belonging to Hurpurshad, Chuckladar of Khyrabad, accompanied by Fukrooddeen Khan* and Bundeh Hussen :—

1. Miss Jackson.
2. Mrs. Captain Greene.
3. Mr. Coldayrah (?) a writer.
4. The stepson of Sergeant-Major Rodgers.†
5. Mr. Carew, of the Shahjehanpore Rosa Factory.

The above-mentioned persons were brought in on bahuls. On their arrival they were placed under a

* Was a Government agent.

† Twenty years of age.

guard of sepoys. At night, a court was assembled to debate on the subject of the prisoners. This court was composed of Captain Oomrao Sing, 6th Regiment Oude Irregular Force; Captain Rugonath Sing, 2nd Regiment Oude Military Police; Captain Imdad Hoosein, 3rd Regiment Oude Military Police; Darogah Wajid Alee, Munnoo Khan Shurfood Dowlah; and it was the wish of all the members that, as these prisoners were of high rank, it would be advisable not only to save their lives, but to treat them with consideration. The court then ordered Wajid Alee, Darogah, to send for Darogah Mirza Hoosein (the steward), and to instruct him to provide everything for their comfort, with the exception of wine. Wajid Alee was also instructed to provide a suitable house for them. It was decided that they shoulrd be lodged in the house in which Nawab Monowu Ood Dowlah was first imprisoned, but it was enjoined that the Nawab should not be allowed to communicate with the English prisoners. But as there were many sepoys of the 22nd Regiment Native Infantry at the above-mentioned house, Meer Wajid Alee thought it advisable to locate them in the Magina Wallee Baradurree (in the Kaiser Bagh). Meer Hussun Alee brought food and tea, as quickly as possible; but, on seeing this, Captain Mukdoon Bux (formerly a subadar in Captain Bunbury's regiment, and always treated by that officer with particular kindness) placed a guard over the Europeans, and strictly forbad any of the durbar officials having communication with them. Food, however, was still sent to the poor prisoners. On the third day of their arrival at Lucknow, after an unsuccessful attack on the Alumbagh, Mukdoon Bux ordered the prisoners to be brought out, and, taking them towards a nullah near the Tara Kothee (Observatory), on the road to Secunder Bagh, cruelly murdered them. Mrs. Greene and Miss Jackson were brutally dragged along to the place of execution. Twenty-two persons were this day murdered; amongst these five were Mahomedans (and of these one, Mahomed Khan, kotwal of the city), the remainder were Europeans and Eurasians. After the foul murder the bodies were thrown into the river.

The whole of the official and authentic information, now in the possession of the local Government, regarding the fate of those of our countrymen and countrywomen who perished in the mutiny in Oude, is here completed.

Nothing more of an authentic character is known.

It may be interesting to observe that but very few relics of European property have been recovered in

Oude; in some instances, property has been found on sepoys who were slain in action; but the great bulk of European property, such as furniture, horses, carriages, &c., has not been recovered. Most probably, as the country was gradually re-conquered, so the holders of English property, which they had obtained during the mutiny, became alarmed, and destroyed it.

G. HUTCHINSON, *Captain*,
Military Secretary to the Chief Commissioner, Oude.

THE END.

London: Printed by SMITH, ELDER & Co., Little Green Arbour Court, E.C.